A level in a week

Zoe Keeling and Cherie Rowe,
Abbey Tutorial College
Series editor: Kevin Byrne

Where to find the information you need

Letts Educational
Aldine Place
London W12 8AW
Tel: 0181 740 2266
Fax: 0181 743 8451
e-mail: mail@lettsed.co.uk
website: http://www.lettsed.co.uk

The authors and publisher are grateful to the following for permission to reproduce copyright materials: pages 36-38 © 1954,55 by Tennessee Williams, published by New Directions, reprinted by permission of The University of the South, Sewanee, Tennessee; page 59-60 The Estate of F. Scott Fitzgerald and Bodley Head; page 63 The Estate of Sylvia Plath from Selected Poems Faber & Faber Ltd.; page 83 The Estate of Wilfred Owen and Chatto and Windus.

Every effort has been made to trace copyright holders and obtain their permission for the use of copyright material. The authors and publishers will gladly receive information enabling them to rectify any error or omission in subsequent editions.

First published 1999
Reprinted 1999

British Library Cataloguing in Publication Data
A CIP record for this book is available from the British Library.

ISBN 1 85758 928 9

Editorial, design and production by Hart McLeod, Cambridge

Printed in Great Britain

Letts Educational is the trading name of BPP (Letts Educational) Ltd

Revision and exam technique: essay writing

10 minutes

Test your knowledge

1 If you see an essay title that you have never tackled before, do not _____!

2 You should analyse the _____ _____ of an essay title so that you understand exactly what the question means.

3 Once you have understood the title, you should make an essay _____.

4 The _____ of your essay will re-word the title and give an indication of your line of argument.

5 Each paragraph in your essay should follow a three step process:
- make a _____
- support it with a _____ or close _____ _____
- make the point _____ to _____ the question.

6 In the _____ you should summarise the argument of your essay, drawing together an answer to the question, possibly including your own personal response.

7 True or false?
It is a good idea to learn essays off by heart – something similar will come up in the exam.

✔ If you got them all right, skip to page 5

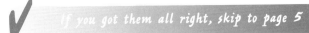

1

Revision and exam technique: essay writing

30 minutes

Improve your knowledge

An essay is an opportunity for you to express your **ideas, thoughts** and **feelings** about a text. There are no right or wrong answers. So that the examiner can understand your ideas, you must write them in a **logical**, understandable way, hence the importance of writing **coherent, well-constructed** essays.

Writing an essay is like building a house. You must:

- **analyse** the question to understand exactly what type of house to build
- **plan** carefully to make sure that you know what materials to use to raise strong foundations
- have a clear idea about how you intend to build the house
- **lay** the bricks in a logical order to provide a coherent structure.

The finished house shows your clear understanding and appreciation of the fabric and construction of the building.

1 If you know your text well, you can answer any question given to you. It is very tempting to presume that if you haven't done the essay title before, you can't do it. You should remember that the same question can be asked in many different ways; it is your job to think on your feet and decipher exactly what the question is asking you.

2 You must take some time to analyse and understand the **key words** in the essay title – you can underline them if that helps. It is only then that you will know exactly what the question is asking you. If you find this hard, try putting the words into other contexts or try to define what the word *doesn't* mean. Once you have analysed the words in the title, re-phrase the title in your own words. Make sure that you consider all the parts of the question.

don't re-tell the plot

don't use long words – just write clearly

always answer the question!

know your text backwards!

plan before you write

assume that your examiner has read the text!

write your plan in your exam answer booklet

3 An essay plan ensures that your answer is well constructed – an argument instead of arbitrary jottings. An essay should contain:

- an introduction
- an argument
- a conclusion.

Since most questions ask you to agree or disagree with a statement, you can plan your essay in two columns. You will need to list in the 'agree' column all the points you can think of which support the statement. In the 'disagree' column you will need to include all the points that prove the opposite. You may find that one particular point supports both sides, in that an event or character can be seen in several ways. This is all right. Showing that you can see both sides of a story is a good thing; you may identify both viewpoints and then take one as your preferred. Once you have completed the columns, you will probably notice that one column is longer than the other. This tends to indicate the answer to the question in that if you cannot think of many points to agree with the title, plainly, you don't!

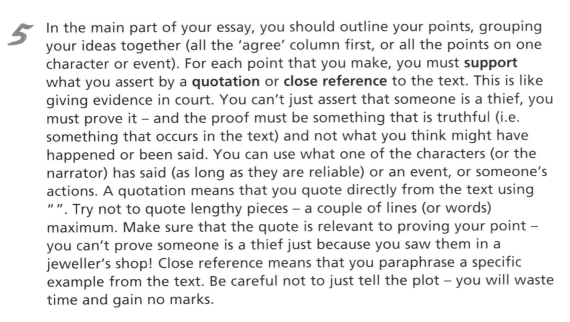

this three step process will ensure that your points are always well supported and that they are relevant to answering the questions. It will be very difficult for you to 'wander off the subject'!

4 Once you have planned carefully, you need to write an introduction, which should have two parts to it.

- Show the examiner that you understand the **meaning** of the question by re-wording the title and re-phrasing the meaning.
- Give the examiner some indication of the **structure** of your essay or essay plan.

5 In the main part of your essay, you should outline your points, grouping your ideas together (all the 'agree' column first, or all the points on one character or event). For each point that you make, you must **support** what you assert by a **quotation** or **close reference** to the text. This is like giving evidence in court. You can't just assert that someone is a thief, you must prove it – and the proof must be something that is truthful (i.e. something that occurs in the text) and not what you think might have happened or been said. You can use what one of the characters (or the narrator) has said (as long as they are reliable) or an event, or someone's actions. A quotation means that you quote directly from the text using " ". Try not to quote lengthy pieces – a couple of lines (or words) maximum. Make sure that the quote is relevant to proving your point – you can't prove someone is a thief just because you saw them in a jeweller's shop! Close reference means that you paraphrase a specific example from the text. Be careful not to just tell the plot – you will waste time and gain no marks.

If you cannot find any proof in the text to support your point, think very carefully about the point you are making. Is it really valid? Lastly, you must make each point relevant to answering the question. Refer back to your essay title and ask yourself how your point has helped you establish an answer to the question.

6   The examiner should be able to understand a **summary** of your answer by reading your **conclusion**. The rest of your essay provides the details and proof. The conclusion should therefore summarise all the key points concisely, each reduced to a single phrase or sentence. You may include a personal response or opinion.

7   Do not try to recycle or learn essays off by heart. Your essay will not be relevant to answering the question and you will lose marks for this, no matter how good your learnt essay is!

Revision and exam technique: essay writing

30 minutes

Use your knowledge

Read the following well-known story:

Once upon a time, a Queen had a daughter, whom she called Snow White. Unfortunately, soon after her child was born, the Queen died. A year later the King married again. The new Queen was very beautiful, but rather vain. She couldn't bear to think that anyone else might be more beautiful than her. The Queen had a magic mirror. Often she stood in front of it and, admiring her own reflection, asked 'Who is the fairest of them all?' The mirror always replied 'You, oh Queen, are the fairest'. The Queen was always extremely happy when she heard this because she knew that the mirror couldn't lie.

One day, the reply from the mirror changed: 'You, oh Queen, are fair, but Snow-White is more lovely'. When the Queen heard this she was very angry and became very jealous of Snow-White. When the Queen's envy became intolerable she asked a huntsman to take Snow-White to the forest and kill her. The huntsman obeyed the Queen, but when Snow-White pleaded for her life, promising never to return to the kingdom, he let her go, knowing that the wild beasts in the forest would no doubt devour her that night anyway.

Snow-White ran as fast as she could until she came to a little cottage which belonged to seven dwarfs. When the dwarfs heard Snow-White's story, they offered her a home if she would cook, wash and clean for them. They warned her that they were out working all day and that if her step-mother were to learn that she were alive, she would try to kill her. 'Let no-one into the house while we are away', they pleaded.

Meanwhile, the Queen had discovered Snow-White was still alive and she was so jealous that she disguised herself as a pedlar and visited the dwarfs' cottage. 'Laces and pretty ribbons for sale!' she cried and Snow-White, tempted by the ribbons, opened the door. Snow-White chose some pretty pink laces which the Queen tied round her so tightly that Snow-White could

5

not breathe and she fell down as if dead. When the dwarfs returned home, they managed to revive her, and, hearing what had happened, again warned Snow-White not to let anyone enter the house.

Of course, once the Queen had discovered that her plan had not worked she quickly set about a new plot. Dressed as a pedlar again, she poisoned a comb and as Snow-White gazed at the pretty object she could not resist letting the pedlar into the cottage. Once the Queen had stuck the comb sharply into Snow-White's head, she fell to the floor, as if dead.

Once more the dwarfs returned and revived Snow-White and begged her never to let anyone enter the house while they were out. However, when the mirror informed the Queen that Snow-White was still alive, the Queen poisoned the red half of an apple and set out, disguised as a farmer's wife, to kill the girl. Once Snow-White saw the apple, she longed to eat it, and did after the Queen had eaten the green half herself. Snow-White fell down dead.

The dwarfs placed her body in a glass coffin on the top of a mountain. One day a passing prince fell in love with her and asked that he might take her away with him. As they carried the coffin down the mountain the apple which had stuck in Snow-White's throat suddenly flew out and she revived. The Prince decided to marry her and Snow-White left the dwarfs and became a princess. The Queen was so angry when she found out what had happened that very soon she died.

1   Write an essay plan for the following question:

'As the sole evil character in *Snow-White*, the step-mother is fully culpable for Snow-White's near demise.' How far do you agree with this statement?

Answers on page 84

Revision and exam technique: style toolbox

10 minutes

Test your knowledge

1. Underline the words that you feel are too colloquial/informal for a good essay style, or are over-used, in the following example:

   'Oberon won't let Titania have the changeling child, which is a bit tight. Then Oberon gets Puck to make Titania make a complete idiot of herself with Bottom and I'm sure she was completely mortified when she came to.'

2. Underline all the words that indicate a first person voice:

   'In my opinion, Prospero uses his magic to ill effect, and I think that it is Miranda, Ariel and Caliban who suffer. It seems to me that his behaviour is utterly selfish.'

3. Write the full versions of the following abbreviations:

   (a) can't   (b) didn't   (c) shouldn't   (d) I'll   (e) we're   (f) I'd   (g) they've

4. Change the following sentence into the present tense:

   '*Macbeth* was a tragedy written by Shakespeare, in which the hero returned from a victorious battle, encountered three witches and then became Thane of Cawdor, as they had prophesied.'

5. Connect the correct linguistic pointers with the appropriate sentences: (i) but (ii) therefore   (iii) however

   (a) The novel was accused by critics of triviality, _____ it was generally well received.
   (b) Hippolyta was the Queen of the Amazons and is accordingly a powerful female figure. _____ her capture by Theseus symbolises the dominance of men over women.
   (c) Mary is a kind, gentle character who refuses Chiltern's offer of marriage sympathetically. Margaret, _____, rebuffs him with a cruel severity.

Answers

1 too colloquial – won't, a bit tight, gets, complete idiot, I'm, mortified, came to/over-used – make, complete/completely   2 my opinion, I think, seems to me   3 (a) cannot (b) did not (c) should not (d) I will (e) we are (f) I had (g) they have   4 '*Macbeth* is a tragedy written by Shakespeare, in which the hero returns from a victorious battle, encounters three witches and then becomes Thane of Cawdor, as they had prophesied.'   5 a (i), b (ii), c (iii)

If you got them all right, skip to page 10

7

Revision and exam technique: style toolbox

30 minutes

Improve your knowledge

Your choice of language, fluency of sentence structure and clarity of expression are an important part of your essay writing and will gain or lose you marks accordingly. You should therefore try to adopt a suitable style for writing your essays. If you read essays written by literary critics (preferably on the texts that you are studying) you will quickly accumulate an understanding of the type of language and grammar employed to express **literary criticism**.

1   Try to choose your words carefully, so that they best and most precisely express what you want to communicate. Avoid using slang or colloquialisms (vocabulary that you would use in speech, but not in formal writing) e.g. 'It was *daft* of him to assume that . . . ' or 'He must have been *bonkers* to *go along* with it'. Above all, language exists as a means of **communication**, so it is better to express your ideas coherently than misuse words that you do not really understand. Try not to repeat or over-use particular words.

2   Try not to over-use the first person in your narrative – 'I think . . . ', 'In my opinion . . . ', It seems to me . . . '. Express your ideas in a more **objective fashion**. 'This character seems to be selfish because . . . ' or 'It appears that the character is selfish when . . . '.

3   Try to avoid using abbreviations for words (don't, won't, couldn't, e.g., i.e.). Numbers should be written in words.

4   You should write about texts in the present rather than the past tense ('Chapter One introduces the theme of . . . ' rather than 'Chapter One introduced the theme of . . . ').

spell the author/poet/ playwright's name correctly!

spell the characters' names correctly!

try to avoid 'get' and 'got' – replace with any other verb

try not to use 'a lot' – replace with 'many'

construct the sentence in your head before you write it

read as much and widely as possible

read and mark your friends' essays

5 Be aware of words in the English language which function as **linguistic pointers** to your reader. These words do not provide meaning to the content or subject of your essay, but they do help your reader understand how you are expressing and organising your ideas and arguments in your text. Using the correct linguistic pointers also helps your essay to be more cohesive and flowing.

- When you want to write about a situation and its consequences, you should use 'if' at the beginning of the sentence. Make sure that you include a second clause which states the consequence, usually introduced by the word 'then'.

  '**If** Leo had not read the unsealed letter, **then** he might never have guessed the true nature of Marian and Ted's relationship.'

- If you want to make two statements contrast with each other within a sentence, you can use the following words: although, but, yet, whereas, whilst.

  'Hamlet talks of suicide, **although** he never acts on this impulse.'

  'Ophelia pleads with her father to allow her to continue her relationship with Hamlet, **but** he refuses.'

  'Gertrude appears to be an affectionate, almost fawning mother, **yet** she does nothing to protect Hamlet.'

  'Polonius thinks that Hamlet is mad, **whereas** Hamlet has in fact put on an "antic disposition"'.

  'Claudius is an excellent, fast-acting monarch, **whilst** Hamlet is indecisive and hesitant.'

- If you want to contrast the meaning of two separate sentences, you can start the second sentence with the word 'however':

  'At the start of the novel, Pip possesses a sensitive and caring nature. **However**, once he has received his fortune, his character changes.'

- If a second sentence draws its conclusion from a previous sentence, you may start the second sentence with 'therefore':

  'Leo has come from a sheltered background with little exposure to, or education in, social behaviour. **Therefore**, when he visits Brandham Hall, he finds himself in a confusing environment with its set codes of behaviour.'

✔ *Now learn how to use your knowledge*

9

Revision and exam technique: style toolbox

Use your knowledge

1 Lucy needs some help with her essay style. Read the excerpt from her essay below and underline any words or phrases that you feel are inappropriate for a good essay and suggest suitable alternatives:

On: Brontë's *Wuthering Heights*

The author tried to write so that my feelings are affected by Heathcliffe's feelings. Heathcliffe doesn't care much for Cathy's husband turning up to find him at her grave. Cathy was the only thing that Heathclif cared about and now she's dead nothing seems to matter.

I feel the poet showed Heathcliff's desperate need to be near Cathy; his passion for her is so strong, he can't rest without her. Heathcliffe's desperation to see Cathy again makes me feel sick – he should have thought of all of this before. Having said this, I did feel a bit emotional towards Heathclif and his inability to let go.

Bronte's description of Heathcliff digging up the grave was quite descriptive. Therefore even when Heathclif is doing this, he reckoned that Cathy is not at peace because he heard something like a sigh. At this stage Bronte showed that Heathcliffe's unhappiness is because Cathy has gone and all he wants to do is see her again, or be buried with her so that they can be together again.

Once again, one's feelings turn back to sadness because of the effect Bronte has achieved. The different types of power that Bronte manages to achieve make this particular passage very gripping. I feel that the poet has done a good job of describing all the emotions involved and I really wish that Cathy could have come back, just like Heathclif wanted.

Answers on page 85

Revision and exam technique: preparing your text

60 minutes

The questions below require a very good knowledge of your set text – the starting point for exam success.

1 Name the key characters in your text and the characters that you feel are secondary to the plot.

2 What are the key themes of the text? How are they developed throughout the text?

3 For each of the characters and themes, provide four quotes that might help you explain your ideas about them in an essay.

4 Name as many contrasts as you can think of in your text. Why do you think that these contrasts exist and what effects do they have on your understanding of the text?

5 What types of imagery and symbolism are used within your text?

6 What century is your text set in? What was happening historically at the time?

7 Who is your writer? When were they born and what motivated and inspired them to write?

Answers

The answers to all of these questions rely on your knowledge and careful study of your set text. A visit to a good library will provide you with bibliographies of your writer, books of criticism on your text and the peace and quiet you need to read your text thoroughly!

If you got them all right, skip to page 15

Revision and exam technique: preparing your text

45 minutes

Improve your knowledge

1 Many exam boards now allow A-level students to take their texts into the exam room with them. This is called an 'open book' exam. There are obvious advantages to this – it means that you do not have to learn quotes and you have the reassurance that the book is right there in front of you! There are, however, disadvantages. Many students forget the importance of knowing their texts well and waste much of their exam time flicking through pages to refresh their memory or find an appropriate quote.

2/3 Some exam boards do not allow students to take books into the exam room and others have adopted a mixed policy. Students studying with these boards will need to **learn** quotes. This can be time consuming and demanding on the memory. Some students are so concerned with using all their hard learnt quotes that they base the structure of their essays around including as many as possible!

annotate your text carefully

However, taking the time to **identifying key quotes** demands that you pay close attention to the details of your text and this is one of the best ways to prepare and revise your texts effectively.

identify key extracts

You will need to divide your text into **manageable chunks**. The following points should help you achieve this:

- **Follow the development** of each of the characters from the beginning of the text through to the end. Establish how the characters have developed and evolved and what incidents or comments within the text reveal these changes.

12

- **Identify the themes**, or recurring ideas, that run through the text. Look closely at how these ideas are developed and what possible moral standpoints are taken. Are the themes conveyed subtly or blatantly?
- Once you have identified the key themes and characters, **designate** each a colour. As you re-read the text, **underline** useful quotes or relevant sections in the appropriate colour. This will ensure that you can find quotes in the text easily during an exam, but it will also enable you to gather information about your text quickly for revision and practice essays.

colour code your quotes

summarise the contents of each chapter

4 Having become a master of the details of the text (!) you should try to draw together some coherent ideas about the text as a whole. Consider aspects of the text such as **contrasts**. Check the presentation of male and female characters – are all the males dominant and all the females submissive, or do contrasts within each gender exist? It can be helpful to think about the battle between good and evil, sophistication and simplicity, strong versus weak and other conflicts.

5 You must carefully examine the use of language in the text. You should look at the **level of formality**, the **overall structure** of the text and the **use of imagery**. Collect together the adjectives and adverbs used to describe each of the characters – you may find that the writer has adopted particular types of words to describe them. You may also find it useful to **study the language** used by the characters themselves, when they talk with each other and, in novels, when the narrator allows **internal monologue**. Symbolism, such as use of colours, setting, environment and weather to mirror emotions or the events of the plot, is also important.

know the chronology of the plot

6 You must **understand the era** in which your text is set. Identify the century and date and complete some investigations into the **important historical events** of the period. Try to discover the social and economic climate of the age, what sort of class system was in operation, whether the country was at war or peace, what people worried about and how concerned the political body in charge were about these worries. A historic perspective of your text is important for you not to make crucial errors. You must place the events of the text in their appropriate era – you cannot judge a piece of writing from the eighteenth century by today's social and moral standards.

look for symbols

what's the date?

7 You should make some attempt to **research the life** of your author/poet/playwright. Consider the influencing factors in their lives, what concerned them, their key moral issues, their personal life and relationships. It is more than likely that at least some of these are mirrored or revealed in your text. You will not be required to refer to, or write, a biography of the author in the exam, but you can use this information to gain a broader understanding of the text and it will help you **empathise** with the text and its writer.

who is this writer?

✓ *Now learn how to use your knowledge*

Revision and exam technique: preparing your text

30 minutes

1   Choose one of the **key characters** in the text and answer the questions below:

(a) When do you first meet the character and how does the language of the text influence your perception of their character?

(b) How does a second meeting change any of your ideas about their personality? Does anything that they do or say sway your opinion?

(c) For each of the consequent times that the character appears, make a note of the presentation of the character and any changes that you feel occur, particularly the last time that you see them.

(d) Make a list of what the other characters have said about this character, including the narrator – how reliable is what they have said and what information does this give you about the character?

(e) Write one paragraph describing how this character undergoes change throughout the text, using the details of the text to support your points.

2   Identify one of the **themes** of the text and answer the following questions:

(a) When did the theme first become apparent – was this a subtle indication or a blatant assertion?

(b) When is the theme next presented? Does the time or place affect your understanding of the handling of the theme?

(c) As the text progresses, how does the theme develop? Does one character have any particular influence on the theme's progress? If so, why do you think that this is?

3 Remind yourself of the **contrasts** within the text:

(a) Do the contrasts become more or less extreme as the text progresses?
(b) What do the contrasts tell you about the themes or characters in the text?
(c) Do any of the contrasts become resolved?

4 Concentrating on the **language** of the text, consider the following points:

(a) How does the level of formality of the writing affect your reading of the text? Does the level of formality reflect the character of your narrator, or the seriousness of the tone? Does it create any sense of irony?
(b) Is there any symmetry in the structure of the plot that perhaps reflects the subject matter or themes of the text? Look at the locations of, and participants in, events at the beginning and end of the text.

5 Consider the **historical period** of the text:

(a) How is the period setting established and in what ways is the period different to the one that you live in? You should consider costume, etiquette, class, social expectation, education and standard of living.
(b) In what ways do the concerns of the period become apparent within the text? Sometimes you will find that this is manifested in the portrayal of the suffering of groups of people within the story – miners (D. H. Lawrence), factory workers (Elizabeth Gaskell), soldiers (Wilfred Owen), and children (Charles Dickens).

6 Having read about the **life of your writer**, consider the following points:

(a) What aspects of the writer's life are reflected in the subject matter of the text?
(b) Are there any parallel episodes in the events of the writer's life and that of the text?
(c) How have the writer's real-life relationships – perhaps an unhappy marriage or the loss of someone close to them – influenced their depiction of relationships within the text?

Answers on page 86

Drama toolbox

Test your knowledge

15 minutes

1 Examiners expect me to analyse the playwright's use of dramatic _____ and the _____ upon the audience.

2 There are eight different genres of drama, three of which are _____, _____, and _____.

3 The organisation of the actions of the characters is called the _____.

4 When I am analysing the characters in my plays I should be looking at the following key features:

(a) Function which is _____.

(b) Role which is the _____.

(c) Actions which are _____.

(d) Interactions which are _____.

(e) Speech which consists of _____.

(f) Emotion which reveals _____.

(g) Response which is the way the _____.

5 I need to closely analyse the speech of the characters because it tells me _____. The features of speech I should be looking at are _____, rhythm, _____, mood and _____.

6 When I am discussing the actions of a character I should be considering how well the action relates to the _____, the _____ or silence that accompanies the action and the _____ of the other characters to the action.

7 To show the examiner I am interpreting the text as drama I need to consider the _____ of the play. This includes analysis of _____, lighting, _____ and scenery.

Answers

1 techniques, effect   2 you could have had comedy, tragedy, tragicomedy, romance, Shakespearean, Jacobean, 19th century or modern   3 plot   4 (a) their purpose in the plot (b) relationships with other characters (c) behaviour (d) actions affecting other characters (e) what they say and how they say it (f) feelings and demonstrations of feelings (g) audience react to the character   5 the feelings of the characters, tone, images, structure   6 plot, dialogue, response   7 staging, costume, directions

✓ *If you got them all right, skip to page 23*

Drama toolbox

Improve your knowledge

15 minutes

1 **Drama** is the art of make believe and you must focus on how the dramatist creates and maintains the illusion and how effective the illusion is. Remember that drama:

- entertains and instructs
- imitates life
- presents an illusion.

The audience participates in maintaining the illusion by suspending their disbelief: you know that the performance is not real, but an effective dramatist will make you engage with the characters and the action, often moving your emotions from fear to joy. Your essay should show:

remember: construction + effects

- your understanding of the how the drama is constructed
- analysis of dramatic effects and techniques.

An effective essay will consider **plot**, **actions and speech of the characters**, **setting** and the **audience's response**.

2

Genre	Important Features
Comedy	Characters' difficulties promote amusement. Audience knows no great disaster will occur. Ends happily for the characters.
Tragedy	Serious, important actions of protagonist results in disaster. Protagonist is mixture of good and evil. Catastrophe is greater than what seems to be just.
Tragicomedy	Mixture of tragedy and comedy. Tragic moments relieved by comedy. Audience laughs uneasily; funny yet sardonic.
Romance	Harmful deed creates distress and absence. New factor emanates that transforms old situation. Mercy and forgiveness resolves; reconciliation results.

Period	Important Features
Shakespearean	Interest in human nature, experience and dilemmas. Often interweaves plot and sub-plot.
Jacobean	Subversive, shows humanity to be defective, often debauched, susceptible to vice, revenge and corruption.
Late nineteenth century	Subversive, rejection of Victorian values. Socialism, science and philosophy are common themes. Use of paradoxical wit to disturb traditional beliefs and values.
Modern	Innovation, alternative and unconventional use of plot structure, characters and setting.

3 Plot structure

Put simply, the plot is what the characters do. Examiners are interested in your appreciation of the importance of the **way dramatists organise their plots.** Aristotle and Freytag have both described the organisation of a play by identifying key moments in the dramatic action:

Exposition	Exposition	Background information explains how the characters arrived at their situation.
Dramatic incitement	Suspense	Incident which begins the main action, builds tension.
Complication	Rising action	Main action where characters respond to the dramatic incitement.
Crisis	Climax	Pinnacle of the action, greatest revelation experience by protagonist, appreciation of circumstances.
Resolution	Falling action	The resolution may determine issues and answer questions. It may also reflect the beginning of the play, making the plot circular.

remember: plot = organisation

Dénouement Complications are unknotted. This may involve a reversal (**peripety**) in the protagonist's fortunes as they make a discovery (**anagnorisis**) of something vitally important that they never knew before.

Plots can also be **single** or **interrelated**.

- **Single** plots: often concentrated and immensely intense.
- **Interrelated** plot will often have a **sub-plot** which mirrors and reflects the main plot.

Pace is the speed at which the action (plot) progresses. An effective dramatist changes the pace of the play with pauses followed by intense, sustained action. Think about how the pace relates to the action and creation of atmosphere in the play. Plot is dependent on character and often arises from conflict between characters.

4 Characters

Analysis of characters in a drama text is similar to that in a prose text. In drama, everything you know about a character comes from what you see: **actions** and what you hear: **speech**. When analysing your characters you should consider the following features: (remember them as **FRAISER**)

- **Function** – purpose in plot
- **Role** – dynamics of relationships with other characters
- **Actions** – what the character does and their behaviour
- **Interactions** – how other characters relate to them and vice versa
- **Speech** – what they say, how they say it, key speeches, soliloquies
- **Emotion** – what they feel and how they demonstrate it
- **Response** – how the audience is encouraged to relate to the character.

5 Speech

Speech tells the story through **revealing the character, advancing the action** and **introducing and developing themes.** Dramatists alternate between using verse and prose in the speech of their characters. Traditionally, verse is used by noble or main characters whereas prose is used to denote characters of low social standing. The decision to convey speech through verse elevates the speaker's position and enhances what they have to say. The use of prose may be used to convey matter of fact comments.

Dialogue occurs between characters and you should look for what the exchange reveals about each character, how it relates to the plot and whether any deception or insight into a character's motives is revealed.

Soliloquy is when a character is the only speaker, allowing the audience a truthful, deeper insight as there is no point lying to oneself.

Speech is an indicator of the individual, consider how well you know your best friend's speech. Attempt to analyse the language of the main characters using these key terms:

- **Tone** – the emotions conveyed
- **Rhythm** – the movement and pace of the lines
- **Imagery** – use of metaphors, similes or recurring images
- **Mood** – the atmosphere the lines create
- **Structure** – the form of the speech (verse or prose for example).

learn the TRIMS method

6 Actions

The actions of a character are simply what he or she does. Always consider their actions in relation to the plot, speech and other characters. For example, in *The Changeling* by Middleton and Rowley, a significant action is when De Flores, a wicked servant who is in love with Beatrice, produces the finger of a man whom her father intended her to marry against her wishes.

> De Flores: But it was sent somewhat unwillingly;
> I could not get the ring without the finger.
> [*shows her the finger*]
> Beatrice: Bless me! What hast thou done?

De Flores reveals that he thinks nothing of murder, especially as he lusts for Beatrice. Beatrice has requested and paid him to murder Alonzo. Her reaction to De Flores's action is one of horror. The audience realises the true extent of her and De Flores's evil at the same time she does.

7 Staging

The stage directions are vital and you should consider all stage directions because they are the dramatist's comments about the action. Many students often ignore the stage directions altogether, thus failing to show the examiner how much they appreciate the text as a dramatic form. Tennessee Williams's stage directions are very specific and extremely detailed which assist in interpreting the action on stage. Make notes on how the following influence the action in the play you are studying:

visualise your play – be the director!

- costume
- lighting
- directions
- scenery.

Common exam questions

Always remember that examiners are interested in your response but ensure it is **relevant** to the question and **supported** by textual evidence. Here are some key words often used in questions about drama with tips on how to answer them.

Effective: the question will direct you to a specific action or technique in the play. (Is the ending effective? Is the use of flashback effective?) Explain whether it is effective or not and how the effect is achieved through plot, characters' actions and speech and setting.

Character: use **FRAISER** in your response to the question. Don't write a generalised character summary but **tailor** your answer to the question.

Context: closely analyse the section of the play, noting how it relates to the overall play.

exam tips

✓ *Now learn how to use your knowledge*

Drama toolbox

Use your knowledge

Choose one of your examination plays to answer the following questions. The answers are to guide you and ensure you have addressed the relevant areas.

1 The central purpose of the play I am studying is to _____.

2 This play was written in the (a) _____ period and has the following features (b) _____ , (c) _____ , (d) _____. The genre this play fits into best is (e) _____ because (f) _____.

3 Fill in the table with references from your play to highlight the five key moments in the plot:

Exposition		
Dramatic incitement	or	Suspense
Complication	or	Rising action
Crisis	or	Climax
Resolution	or	Falling action

transfer your charts onto record cards

4 For each main character summarise their features by filling in the following table:

Feature	Evidence	Comment
Function		
Role		
Actions		
Interactions		
Speech		
Emotion		
Response		

*decorate your room with colour **A3** charts*

 5 For each main character summarise the features of their speech:

Feature	Evidence	Comment
Tone		
Rhythm		
Idioms		
Mood		
Syntax		

Answers on page 86

Shakespeare

Test your knowledge

30 minutes

1. Shakespeare was writing in the _____ period and his audience consisted of *noblemen/rich and poor citizens/men only*.

2. Shakespeare drew on a variety of genres in writing his plays: _____, _____, _____, _____ _____ and _____ .

3. In Shakespeare I need to analyse the _____, role, _____ interactions, _____, emotion and _____ of the main characters.

4. Annotate and analyse the following speech from *King Lear*:

   > Blow winds, and crack your cheeks! Rage, blow,
   >   You cataracts and hurricanoes, spout
   > Till you have drenched our steeples, drowned our cocks
   > You sulph'rous and thought executing fires,
   > Vaunt-couriers of oak cleaving thunderbolts
   > Singe my white head; and thou all shaking thunder,
   > Strike flat the thick rotundity o' th' world,
   > Crack nature's moulds, all germens spill at once
   > That makes ingrateful man.

5. To examine the actions of a character I need to look for the _____ of the character. These come from the temperament, _____ and moral nature of the character.

6. A director will construct the staging according to their _____ of the play. The choice of costume, lighting, time and historical setting and _____ affects the way the audience view the play.

If you got them all right, skip to page 30

Shakespeare

Improve your knowledge

60 minutes

1 Shakespeare was writing in the Elizabethan age and among his contemporaries are Marlowe, Tourneur, Webster and Jonson. Shakespeare's audience would be around 2500 people from all social classes and ages. Remember to use the extensive **footnotes** to help you appreciate some of the references that Shakespeare's audience would have been familiar with.

2 **Genres in Shakespeare's plays**

Genre	Key features	Examples
Tragedy	Eponymous (and flawed) hero. Action results in disruption. Chaos results, excessive emotions. Breakdown of social morality and order. Climax is death of hero. Order is restored.	*King Lear* *Othello* *Hamlet* *Romeo and Juliet*
History	Crisis of historical figure. Affects order of the state. Exploration of notion of kingship. Rebels contribute to chaos. Heroes are shown to be imperfect.	*Richard II* *Henry IV (Part 1)* *Henry IV (Part 2)* *Henry V* *Antony and Cleopatra* *Coriolanus* *Julius Caesar*
Comedy	Foolish behaviour. Fantasy or dreamlike situations. Normal life and love. Mischance and predicaments result in confusion. Confusion resolved. Happy ending with united lovers.	*Twelfth Night* *Love's Labour's Lost* *Much Ado About Nothing* *As You Like It*

Genre	Key features	Examples
Problem comedy	Dark serious tone. Noble characters revealed to be flawed. Ambiguous characters. Unsettling issues raised. Disorder: state or personal Melancholy realistic environment.	*Measure for Measure* *All's Well That Ends Well* *Troilus and Cressida*
Romance	Noble family. Harmful or erroneous deed. Distress and absence. New factor emanates that transforms old situation. Mercy and forgiveness resolves reconciliation.	*Cymbeline* *The Winter's Tale* *The Tempest*

3 A summary of a character analysis of Lady Macbeth:

- **Function** – reveals Macbeth's weakness, provides alternative view of hero.
- **Role** – catalyst for Macbeth's murder of King Duncan.
- **Action** – significant 'unsexing' of female attributes to accomplish deed, resonant of the witches' actions.
- **Interaction** – Macbeth's responses reveal her to be a powerful and efficacious character before the murder of Duncan. After the deed Macbeth increasingly alienates himself which results in an increase in her own personal torment until her suicide.
- **Speech** – similar to witches' by use of invocations and chants, forceful and challenging language in dialogue with Macbeth, disintegrates to incoherent ramblings representing the turmoil of her mind.
- **Emotions** – demonstrates passion, cruelty, love and courage.
- **Response** – audiences have responded to Lady Macbeth as an evil hag, akin to the witches, as a supportive and passionate wife and as a woman scarred by the loss of a child.

4 Character speech

Shakespeare employs a variety of speech in his plays from **blank verse**, **prose, iambic pentameter**, in **fragmented language, poetic verse** to **rhetoric, paradoxical speech** and **wit**. Whatever device is being used it is for a purpose. Always state why the character's speech is constructed in this way.

Tone ──────── Blow, winds, and crack your cheeks! Rage, blow,
    You cataracts and hurricanoes, spout ──────────── *rhythm*
    Till you have drenched our steeples, drowned our cocks! ── *enjambment*
    You sulph'rous and thought executing fires,   *(run on lines)*
    Vaunt-couriers of <u>oak-cleaving thunderbolts</u>
Imagery ──────── <u>Singe my white head; and thou all-shaking thunder,</u>
    <u>Strike flat the thick rotundity o' th' world,</u>
    Crack nature's moulds, all germens spill at once
    That makes ingrateful man.

- **Tone** – anger and rage of a powerful man evident through the imperative commands and direct verbs.
- **Rhythm** – begins slowly and purposefully, increases and gains momentum to match the destructive imagery of the storm, culminates in short, staccato words in the last line.
- **Imagery** – nature condemning the earth. Recurring images of destruction and dividing ('crack', 'drenched', 'drowned', 'thought executing', 'cleaving', 'singe', 'strike flat', 'spill') which climax in a curse for the destruction of the human race.
- **Mood** – fearful, full of vengeance.
- **Structure** – imperative commands in verse, last line is short emphasising the venom and wrath Lear feels.

5 A character's actions are directed by the following:

- temperament
- desires   →   motivations   →   actions
- moral nature.

When you are explaining why a character behaves in the way they do, consider what you know about their nature (**temperament**), what they want (**desires**) and their ethics (**moral nature**). Some characters will change throughout the play (King Lear) whilst other characters remain static (Prospero in *The Tempest*, The Duke in *Measure for Measure*).

Each action has an effect – a reaction. When you are examining a significant action consider also how other characters respond to the action.

6 Commenting on the staging in a Shakespearean play informs an examiner that you understand and appreciate the construction of the text as a piece of drama. Look at the following comments on different aspects of staging:

- **Costume** – used to represent mistaken identities in *The Comedy of Errors*, *A Midsummer Night's Dream*.
- **Scenery** – Athenian wood is an idyllic contrast to the severity of Theseus's court in *A Midsummer Night's Dream*. The storm scenes in *King Lear* heighten the dramatic tension through pathetic fallacy.
- **Lighting** – in the dagger scene in *Macbeth* emphasises the evil about to be committed.
- **Stage directions** – often limited in Shakespeare's plays and left to the director to decide and implement.
- **Time/place** – history plays are often performed in modern day settings to highlight features. Consider why the director has chosen to present the play in a particular period or in a particular location.

Shakespeare

90 minutes

Use your knowledge

1 The genre of the Shakespeare play I am studying is _____.

The evidence for this can be summarised as follows:

Key feature	Comments and textual evidence

2 Make a summary chart for each main character:

Character	Comments and textual evidence
F:	
R:	
A:	
I:	
S:	
E:	
R:	

3 Make a summary speech chart for each main character:

Character	Comments and textual evidence
T	
R	
I	
M	
S	

(Hints)

4 Complete the table to examine the actions of each main character.

Character:

Action	Motivation	Evidence

look for evidence of their:
• temperament
• desires
• moral nature

5 The following physical features of the play I have seen performed were:

Physical Feature	Description	Effect on interpretation
Costume		
Lighting		
Scenery		
Stage directions		
Time		
Place		

borrow the plays from your central library or school

Answers on page 86

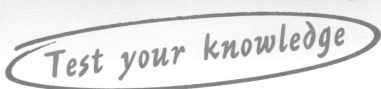

Modern drama

Test your knowledge

15 minutes

1 Modern dramatists are more _____ in their exploration and presentation of human experience than traditional dramatists. This is noticeable in the organisation of _____, the choice of the _____ and the _____ of the play.

2 The main effect upon an audience is that they are _____ in the play rather than being mere observers.

3 Modern dramatists often employ the flashback technique which is when _____ or time shifts which are when _____.

4 Modern dramatists often depict the experiences of _____ characters as opposed to traditionally noble characters. The effect on the audience is that they are able to _____ more readily to the dilemmas of the characters.

5 In most modern plays the characters' speech is written in _____.

6 A dramatist can make the action either _____, when you actually see the character do something, or _____, where an action is suggested.

7 The staging in modern drama is often designed to _____ the audience. Dramatists make use of the stage directions to provide _____ about the characters which is not otherwise specified.

If you got them all right, skip to page 39

Modern drama

Improve your knowledge

60 minutes

1 Modern drama can be described as **eclectic**. Playwrights are no longer tied to conventional plot structures, characters, subject matter or even staging. Often the play will **mirror contemporary society**. In the early part of the twentieth century, experimental theatre mirrored the chaos and disruption of the First and Second World Wars.

Features		Examples
Characters: Ordinary rather than traditionally noble characters.	Audience invited to relate to character due to familiar personalities and situations.	Willy Loman in *Death of a Salesman* by Arthur Miller.
Plot: Provokes dramatic responses to twentieth century events.	Plot constructed to challenge society and the audience directly, often through undermining traditional views and attitudes.	*Journey's End* by R. C. Sherriff *An Inspector Calls* by J. B. Priestly.
Staging: Dramatic illusion.	Staging devised to involve audience in the action rather than distancing them.	*Waiting for Godot* by Samuel Beckett.

2 **Plot structure**

Modern dramatists have the freedom to ignore or distort conventional plot structures. This results in innovative and sometimes confusing plots. Any confusion is intentional and is created to force the audience to become active in unravelling the plot or to be more sympathetic with characters who undergo the same confusion. You should note how the plot of your modern play moves and be able to comment on the effect that particular plot structure has.

Look at the opening of *Arcadia* by Tom Stoppard and the comments that follow:

Thomasina: Septimus, what is carnal embrace?

Arcadia is a play that begins *in media res* (in the middle of things) with a question from a 13 year-old to her tutor: 'Septimus, what is carnal embrace?' Immediately Stoppard involves the audience in the action and initiates a relationship between them and the characters. They are encouraged to be sympathetic to the tutor who is placed in a potentially embarrassing situation whilst also being interested in what has prompted the child to ask such a question. Stoppard also creates curiosity because we want to learn what Septimus's answer will be. This abrupt opening is effective in drawing the audience into the play and immediately establishing the main themes of the play; sexual encounters and the search for knowledge. This directly involves the audience in the play and the dilemmas of the characters. The situation here is a common one which an audience can relate to.

3 Dramatic techniques

Flashbacks: this is where the audience is taken back into the past of the play through the reminiscence or regression of the characters. For example: Arthur Miller uses this technique in *Death of a Salesman* to convey to the audience Willy's experience of a successful past as a salesman. This provides a stark contrast with the present, where he is failing. This dramatic device is effective because it allows the audience to understand Willy's motivations and the desires which prompt his actions.

Time shifts: this is where dramatists merge different time periods in one play. For example, in *Arcadia* the events of 1809 run in parallel to the events in our modern society. This allows an audience to see contrasts and similarities between characters. Stoppard effectively merges the two time periods by having literary, mathematical and garden researchers of the present study the events of the past. Their conclusions are often wrong and they comically misinterpret the evidence which produces comedy.

look up the time period in an encyclopaedia

4 Characters

As modern playwrights often use ordinary people as opposed to removed characters such as kings or noblemen you should pay close attention to the dramatist's presentation of the

- Situation
- Personality
- Outcome

for each main character in your play as well as using the **FRAISER** technique. Asking the following questions will widen your interpretation and analysis:

- Does the dramatist invite the audience to view the character as tragic, heroic or comic?
- Is this achieved through presenting the character in an ordinary way that the audience can relate to?

For example, Willy Loman in *Death of a Salesman* is a husband and father who suffers defeat at the hands of progress, economic failure and a changing society. He is motivated by the need to take care of his family and his suicide is tragic as he fails to achieve this.

 Speech

All dramatists subtly reveal aspects of their characters through their speech. Modern dramatists have experimented with dialogue to produce startling effects.

A **TRIMS** table to summarise the speech of Septimus and Thomasina in *Arcadia* could be:

	Septimus	Thomasina
Tone	Confident, flippant, intellectual, matter of fact.	Quizzical, curious, youthful.
Rhythm	Smooth, pauses for effect to enhance comedy and emphasise absurdity of others.	Pauses to consider but often relentless in her search for knowledge. Repetitive questions.
Imagery	Use of Latin phrases suggestive of education and pomposity, sexual innuendoes common.	Innocent vocabulary, perceptions are a result of a childlike outlook. Uses ordinary objects to express difficult concepts.
Mood	Promotes intellectual snobbery, distances self from others.	Adds dynamism through questioning and energy through enthusiasm.
Structure	Prose throughout, often witticisms or intellectual verbal assaults.	Questions feature predominantly.

Now look at how some of these features are evident in Septimus's reply to Thomasina's question at the beginning of *Arcadia*:

'**Septimus**: Carnal embrace is the practice of throwing one's arms around a side of beef.
Thomasina: Is that all?
Septimus: No . . . a shoulder of mutton, a haunch of venison well hugged, an embrace of grouse . . . *caro*, *carnis*; feminine; flesh.'

This response to a potentially embarrassing question is sharp, witty and essentially accurate. Septimus has avoiding referring to sex by defining the phrase etymologically, through Latin. His second line is flippant as he lists possible alternatives to a side of beef. The audience is also aware that Thomasina had expected more for her answer and is disappointed with his curt reply. We should also note that as she questions his reply, she is not easily satisfied.

6 Actions

A character's actions in drama can be **visual** or **metaphorical**. You will either be able to see them do something or what they say will suggest action that may or may not be carried out. Look at the following examples taken from Tennessee Williams's *Cat on a Hot Tin Roof*:

Maggie: 'You know, if I thought you would never, never, *never* make love to me again – I would go downstairs to the kitchen and pick out the longest and sharpest knife I could find and stick it straight into my heart, I swear that I would!

But one thing I don't have is the charm of the defeated, my hat is still in the ring, and I am determined to win!

[*There is the sound of croquet mallets hitting croquet balls.*]

– What is the victory of a cat on a hot tin roof? – I wish I knew . . .

Just staying on it, I guess, as long as she can . . .

[*More croquet sounds*]

Later tonight I'm going to tell you I love you an' maybe by that time you'll be drunk enough to believe me. Yes, they're playing croquet . . . '

Maggie is the subject of the title of the play; she is the cat. The hot tin roof represents the situation she is in; marriage to a man she adores but who ignores her because of his own feelings of guilt towards his dead male friend. The roof is hot because the situation becomes increasingly tense and passionate. In the above extract, Maggie demonstrates her

notice the metaphorical action given to Maggie

commitment and determination to stay on the roof, to stay in the marriage and to force Brick to acknowledge and even return her love. This action is **implied** through her speech and the suggested dramatic action of killing herself. She does not really stand on a hot tin roof; it is Williams's effective metaphor to convey her personality and situation.

An indication of the outcome is evident in the following extract:

Brick: Don't make a fool of yourself.
Margaret: I don't mind makin' a fool of myself over you!
Brick: I mind, Maggie. I feel embarrassed for you.
Margaret: Feel embarrassed! But don't continue my torture. I
            can't live on and on under these circumstances.
Brick: You agreed to –
Margaret: I know but –
Brick: – accept that condition!
Margaret: I can't! I can't! I can't!
   [*She seizes his shoulder.*]
Brick: Let go!
   [*He breaks away from her and seizes the small boudoir chair and
   raises it like a liontamer facing a big circus cat.*
   *Count five. She stares at him with her fist pressed to her mouth,
   then bursts into shrill, almost hysterical laughter. He remains grave
   for a moment, then grins and puts the chair down . . .*]

notice Brick's visual action

Brick's actions emphasise Maggie's cat-like features and his response to her determined actions to demonstrate and consecrate her love for him. Her power at this point of the play has increased as Williams indicates by referring to her as a 'lion'. She invades his personal space and this should be evident visually. Brick is forced to either accept or reject her advances. The intensely physical and animalistic way he responds to her demonstrates the extent and depth of their emotions, although he may not yet recognise this. Maggie's reactions to Brick discloses a release of tension in an extremely powerfully emotional manner as she becomes aware of the extent of Brick's rejection of her.

*think
action
↓
analysis
↓
effect*

7 Staging

The way the playwright wishes to present the drama is often detailed in the **stage directions**. Directors of plays do have a free hand in the way they present a play but the stage directions are vital for an insightful and perceptive appreciation of the play. Note what can be said about the following stage directions.

Big Mama [*terrified, rising*]: Is there? Something? Something? Something that I? Don't – Know?

[*In these few words, this startled, very soft question, Big Mama reviews the history of her 45 years with Big Daddy, her great, almost embarrassingly true-hearted and simple-minded devotion to Big Daddy, who must have had something Brick has, who made himself loved so much by the 'simple expedient' of not loving enough to disturb his charming detachment, also once coupled, like Brick's, with virile beauty. Big Mama has a dignity at this moment: she almost stops being fat.*]

internal thought process

audience reaction to her

relationship with Big Daddy

elevates Big Mama to encourage sympathy

Tennessee Williams's stage directions are very specific and convey details about Big Mama that the audience would not necessarily know. Essentially Williams's careful control of the character's emotions are effected through the stage directions.

Modern drama

Use your knowledge

120 minutes

1. The play I am studying is modern because _____.

2. The audience's response at the end of the play would be _____.

3. The plot devices the dramatist employs are _____ _____ , _____.

4. A table to summarise the characters in the play would be:

Character:	Textual evidence	Analysis
Situation		
Personality		
Outcome		

5. Make a summary speech chart for each main character:

Character	Comments and textual evidence
T	
R	
I	
M	
S	

6. An analysis of the significant actions for each character should refer to which three points?

7. Identify three important features in the staging of your play and comment on how they relate to the main action.

Answers on page 87

Prose toolbox

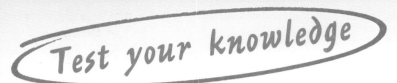

Test your knowledge

10 minutes

1. The _____ of a novel refers to the way in which the events are ordered within the plot.

2. The central ideas or concepts of a novel can be called the _____.

3. The people who participate in the events of the novel can be called _____.

4. Name three types of narrator: _____, _____ and _____.

5. The term used to identify the location of events in a novel is _____ or _____.

6. The _____ _____ of a novel means investigating the era that it is set in.

7. The literary term used to describe a statement which actually means the opposite of what it says is _____.

Prose toolbox

Improve your knowledge

A novel should be just like a good film – it can transport you into a different era, a different country, a different world and depict people and places so vividly that you feel you are really there yourself. A novel is made up of an **extended piece of fictional prose narrative**. The genre is very **flexible**; novels can be long or short and some are factual whilst others are purely fictional. There is no strict subject matter.

Normally, however, you will be asked to study novels that are of a fictional nature and contain several characters who are shown to go through a process of change through various social relationships and some arrangement of narrated events.

1 Structure

Novels can be structured in numerous ways. Check to see if the plot seems to conform to a **formula**, whether it is predictable or reminds you of another novel that you may have read. Is the story told **chronologically**, and if not, in what order is it told? What effect does the order have on the way that you see the events and characters of the novel? Where is the **climax** and is the conflict resolved at the end – is it a happy ending, unhappy or somewhere in between? Is the plot **unified** – is each incident somehow related to some other element in the story?

trace the plot from beginning to end

2 Themes

The theme of a novel is the **central idea** or meaning of the story. Some novels contain several themes. The theme provides a unifying point around which the plot, characters, setting, narrator, symbols and other elements of a story are organised. In some novels, the theme is **explicitly stated**. Most writers however present their themes **implicitly**. Therefore, you will need to read the novel closely to identify themes, and in doing so, you will often see more to the characters and events. Determining the theme of a story can be a difficult task, because all of the story's elements may contribute to its **central idea**. Pay attention to the **title** of the novel – it will often provide a lead to a **major theme** or **focus** on the subject

identify the themes

is there a happy ending?

around which the theme develops. Look for details in the story that have potential for **symbolic meaning**. Carefully consider names, places, objects, minor characters and incidents that may foretell future happenings. Be especially attentive to elements that you did not understand on the first reading. Decide if the protagonist changes or develops some important insights as a result of the action. Carefully examine any generalisations that the narrator or protagonist makes about the events of the story. Be certain that your theme does not focus on only part of the story.

3 Characterisation

Do you particularly identify with the **protagonist**? Who is the protagonist? Do any characters change or develop in the course of the story? Are **flat** or **stock characters** used? Is their behaviour **motivated** and **plausible**? How does the author reveal character? Are they directly described or indirectly presented? Are the characters' names used to convey something about them? What is the purpose of the minor characters? Are they individuals, or do they represent ideas or attitudes?

are the characters likeable?

separate out major and minor characters

4 Narratorial voice

The **narrator** refers to the person who tells the story and how the story is told. What we know and how we feel about the events in a story are shaped by the narrator, the teller of the story. The narrator affects our understanding of the characters' actions by filtering what is told through his or her own perspective. The narrator should not be confused with the author, who has created the narrator as another character in the book. Narrators vary according to their degree of participation in the story:

is the narrator just another character?

(a) Third person narrators – he, she or they do not participate in the action and simply tell the story.
- **Omniscient** – stands outside the events, but is all-knowing and can access characters' thoughts and has knowledge of events happening in different places at the same time.
- **Intrusive** – an omniscient narrator who offers comments on characters and events and sometimes reflects morally.
- **Objective** – the narrator remains outside of all the characters.
(b) First person narrators – use 'I'; are involved either as witnesses or as participants in the events. The reader is restricted to the perceptions, thoughts and feelings of that single character.
- **Reliable narrators** – whose accounts we are obliged to trust.
- **Unreliable narrators**, partial, ill-informed or misleading/distorted.

Narrators can be unreliable for a number of reasons: they might lack self-knowledge or they might be innocent and inexperienced (*The Go-Between*, *Catcher in the Rye*). These narrators lack the sophistication to interpret what they see; they are unreliable because the reader must go beyond their understanding of events to comprehend situations.

Who tells the story? Is it a first person or third person narrator? Does the narrator participate in the action at all? How much does the narrator know and does the point of view change at all in the course of the story? Is the narrator reliable and objective? Does the narrator appear too innocent, emotional or self-deluded to be trusted? Does the author comment directly on the action? If told from a different viewpoint, how would the story change? Would anything be lost?

5 Setting and environment

Is the **setting** important? If it were changed, would the story's action and meaning be significantly different? Is the setting **symbolic**? Are the time, place and atmosphere related to the theme?

locations are important

6 Historical context

It is important to remember that the time or year in which the novel is set is extremely important for you to understand and interpret the text.

7 Language style

This refers to the distinctive manner in which a writer **arranges words** to achieve particular effects. This may include individual **word choice, length of sentence**, their **structure**, **tone** and use of **irony**.

watch out for irony

Diction refers to a writer's choice of words. Because different words evoke different associations in a reader's mind. The writer's choice of words is crucial in controlling the **reader's response**. The diction must be appropriate for the characters and the situations in which the author places them.

Sentence structure is another element of a writer's style. Check to see how complexity or simplicity affects your interpretation of characters and events.

Style reveals tone, the author's implicit attitude toward people, places and events in a story. When we speak, tone is conveyed by our voice or body language. In a literary work, the spoken voice is unavailable; instead, we must rely on the context in which a statement appears to interpret it correctly. If we are sensitive to tone, we can get behind a character and see him or her from the author's perspective.

One of the enduring themes in literature is that things are not always what they seem to be. The unexpected complexity that often surprises us in life is frequently found in literature. Irony is often found when a person says one thing and means the opposite (**sarcasm**). **Situational irony** exists when there is an incongruity between what is expected to happen and what actually happens. The ironic situation creates a distinction between **appearances** and **realities** and brings the reader closer to the central meaning of the story.

Another form of irony occurs when an author allows the audience to know more about a situation than a character knows. This is called **dramatic irony** and it creates a discrepancy about what a character believes or says and what the audience understands to be true.

Prose toolbox

Use your knowledge

**60 minutes**

Think carefully about your set novel and then answer these questions:

1 How is the novel structured and what conclusions have you drawn about the effect of the structure on your interpretation of the text?

2 What do you consider to be the themes of the novel? How are the themes developed throughout the text? What is the significance of the title of the novel?

3 With which character do you empathise and why? How do the characters change during the novel? Are there any dull characters and, if so, why do you think that they are included? Are the minor characters believable?

4 Who is your narrator, and does he or she participate in the action? How much does the narrator know and does his/her point of view change at all in the course of the story? Is the narrator reliable and objective or does he or she appear too innocent, emotional or self-deluded to be trusted? If the story were to be told from one of the other character's viewpoints, how might the story change?

5 How many different locations or settings are there in the novel? Do you feel any of them are symbolic or add depth to your understanding of the novel?

6 In what historical period is the novel set? Apply your understanding of that period to the events and characters of the novel. How does this affect your interpretation of events?

7 How does the diction add to your understanding of the novel? In what parts of the novel does the tone change? Can you identify any ironic comment in the narrative?

*Answers on page 87*

45

The nineteenth-century novel

30 minutes

1. Examiners will expect me to have an understanding of the _____ framework in which my novel was set. The concerns of novelists in the nineteenth century ranged from _____, the rise of Chartism, _____ and _____ to the question of women's rights.

2. The structure of the plot can be governed by _____ or by circumstance.

3. Some prevailing themes of nineteenth-century fiction were _____, _____, and _____.

4. To make effective comments about characterisation I need to focus on _____ and _____, and remember to consider the characters in the _____ of the period the novel was written in.

5. Comment on the narrative voice in the following passage:

   Emma Woodhouse, handsome, clever, and rich, with a comfortable home and happy disposition, seemed to unite some of the best blessings of existence; and had lived nearly twenty-one years in the world with very little to distress or vex her.

6. When I analyse the environment of the novel I need to consider the type of _____ used, the imagery, the use of colour, the use of the five _____ and the tone and _____ that is created.

7. I can learn more about when my examination text was written and the circumstances of the times by reading the _____ in a good edition.

Answers

1 contemporary, socialism, religion, faith 2 character 3 you could have mentioned any of the following: social inequalities, character and environment, realist fiction, the past 4 environment, setting, context 5 see the *Improve your knowledge* notes number 5 in this chapter 6 adjectives, senses, attitude 7 introduction

✓ *If you got them all right, skip to page 50*

The nineteenth-century novel

Improve your knowledge

1 Novelists in the nineteenth century were influenced by the turbulent changes in Victorian life and this is reflected in their fiction. Concerns were varied but were reflected by major events such as:

- **social** – 1834 New Poor Law, burning of Houses of Parliament
- **Industrial Revolution** – urbanisation, rural deprivation
- **science** – Darwin's theory of evolution, man is no longer superior
- **religion** – crisis of faith as a result of evolutionary theory
- **gender** – 1870 Married Women's Property Act, women's rights.

By examining the structure and characters of your novel you should be able to discuss how the novelist resolves or continues to question those concerns.

2 The structure of a novel can be **character** or **circumstance** driven. Ask who or what is responsible for the outcome and whether it is successful or not. The structure of Charles Dickens's *A Christmas Carol* is organised by a reversal of fortune; from negative to positive. The events in Thomas Hardy's novels are a result of a mixture of character, fate and environment whereas Jane Austen's novels are arranged around upper-class society and the duty of the individual.

3 Common themes of nineteenth-century novels are:

- **social inequalities** – authorities and institutions are unjust (Charles Dickens)
- **Industrial Revolution** – conflict, low wages, strikes (Elizabeth Gaskell)
- **character and environment** – mutual influences (Charles Dickens, Thomas Hardy)
- **realist fiction** – independence, injustice (Charlotte Brontë)
- **past** – virtues, morals, rural life (Thomas Hardy, George Eliot).

4 To understand the **characterisation** in your novel, attempt to enter the world of the novel (**environment and setting**) and the world of the writer (**contemporary framework**). By considering events from their perspective you are more ready to sympathise and evaluate their actions more effectively. For example:

> The chief – almost the only – attraction of the young woman's face was its mobility. When she looked down sideways to the girl she became pretty, even handsome, particularly that in the action her features caught slantwise the rays of the strongly coloured sun which made transparencies of her ——— *emphasises* eyelids and nostrils and set her fire on her lips. When she *importance of nature* plodded in the shade of the hedge, silently thinking, she had the hard, half-apathetic expression of one who deems ——— *strongly* anything possible at the hands of Time and Chance except, *related to fate* *often* perhaps, fair play. The first phase was the work of Nature, the *opposed* second probably of civilisation.

5 **Narrative voice**

Emma Woodhouse, handsome, clever, and rich, with a comfortable home and happy disposition, seemed to unite some of the best blessings of existence; and had lived nearly twenty-one years in the world with very little to distress or vex her.

The **narrative voice** here is detached and matter of fact. However, although the details appear to give a positive and attractive picture of Emma, the tone is ironic and you sense that the narrator does not approve of this situation or, initially, of Emma. The word 'seemed' undermines the positive description.

Austen: **subtle ironic detachment** – allows reader to judge and evaluate.
Brontë: **first person narrative** – reader involved in character's dilemmas.
Dickens: **first person and multiple narrative voices, journalistic** – echoes vast array of characters: allows for variety of insights.
Hardy: **omniscient and intrusive** – apathetic which enhances tragedy.

When discussing the narrative voice always state the effect produced.

6 Don't skip over the descriptive passages as they contain vital commentary on the action of the novel. When you annotate your text look for the following:

- **description** – what type of adjectives are used?
- **imagery** – are there metaphors or similes that relate to the action?
- **colour** – how does it contribute to the mood and atmosphere?
- **senses** – does the author conjure images through the senses and why?
- **tone** – what is the attitude and feeling towards the setting?

7 Contemporary framework

Examiners expect some appreciation of the **contemporary framework** in which your examination text was written. This means you need to know **when** your novel was first published and what was happening historically at the time. For example in *The Mayor of Casterbridge* Elizabeth-Jane says 'Then the romance of the sower is gone for good,' in response to a new seed thrower machine. This statement demonstrates the changes in agricultural methods in the nineteenth century, the effects of which led to unemployment and increased poverty. By voicing such a statement through a rational and stoic character such as Elizabeth-Jane, Hardy encourages the reader to take notice of it as a social comment.

Now learn how to use your knowledge

1 Read the following passage and annotate it according to:

(1) concern of the novelist
(2) structure of passage
(3) themes addressed
(4) characterisation
(5) narrative voice
(6) environment and setting
(7) contemporary framework.

Jo sweeps his crossing all day long, unconscious of the link, if any link there be. He sums up his mental condition, when asked a question, by replying that he 'don't know nothink'. He knows that it's hard to keep the mud off the crossing in dirty weather, and harder still to live by doing it. Nobody taught him, even that much; he found it out.

   Jo lives – that is to say, Jo has not yet died – in a ruinous place, known to the like of him by the name of Tom-all-Alone's. It is a black, dilapidated street, avoided by all decent people; where the crazy houses were seized upon, when their decay was far advanced, by some bold vagrants, who, after establishing their own possession, took to letting them out in lodgings. Now, these tumbling tenements contain, by night, a swarm of misery. As on the ruined human wretch, vermin parasites appear, so, these ruined shelters have bred a crowd of foul existence that crawls in and out of gaps in walls and boards; and coils itself to sleep, in maggot numbers, where the rain drips in and comes and goes, fetching and carrying fever, and sowing more evil in its every footprint than Lord Coodle and Sir Thomas Doodle and the Duke of Foodle, and all the fine gentlemen in the office, down to Zoodle, shall set right in five hundred years – though born expressly to do it.

Bleak House Charles Dickens (1853)

Answers on page 88

The modern novel

10 minutes

Test your knowledge

1 The key term which describes literature of the early twentieth century is _____.

2 Some novelists of this period described their character's thought processes as if the reader had entered straight into the character's mind. This technique was called_____ _____ _____.

3 The two famous psychotherapists who had a great influence on twentieth- century literature were _____ and _____.

4 The two words that summarise the feeling of novelists between 1900 and 1930 are _____ and _____.

5 Name two elitist novelists of the early twentieth century.

6 What famous Act in 1870 promoted the education of children aged five to thirteen?

7 Hiroshima and Nagasaki were bombed in the year _____.

8 What key term can be used to describe the literature of the second half of the twentieth century?

9 Name two social groups whose fictional works are increasingly popular today.

If you get them all right, skip to page 54

The modern novel

Improve your knowledge

45 minutes

1 Novelists such as Virginia Woolf, James Joyce and D. H. Lawrence are all prominent figures in the twentieth century, but our present century is a difficult one on which to form judgements, especially since it is so close to our present day. In addition to these problems is the simple fact that much more literature has been produced in the twentieth century than in any other period!

Modernism is one key word which describes the first part of the twentieth century. Modernism is post-Darwinian in that it tries to explain man's place in the world, where religion, social stability and ethics had been called into question. The working of the unconscious mind (Freud) had become important, and as far as literature was concerned, all the traditional forms of writing began to lose their order – a novel may have a beginning, middle and end, but they may not necessarily appear in that order.

when God is gone, what is left?

identify modernistic techniques

define what makes a hero

2 The nature of what made up a fictional hero or heroine was also questioned. Novelists had to find a different way of exploring how people are different and the '**stream of consciousness**' technique was developed to show directly and in depth the experience of individual characters. It followed the thought processes of a character directly, as if the reader had entered the mind of the character and experienced the thoughts as they occurred. This idea relates closely to the impressionism of the visual arts.

question the form of the novel

3 The concept of time also changed as it no longer was seen as a series of separate chronological moments. **Freud** and **Jung**'s influence meant that writers came to believe that people are the embodiment of their memories, that the present is the sum of our past and that the form and style of the novel had to capture and present this understanding.

4 The themes which occupied many of the major novelists from 1900–1930 were that of **loneliness** and **isolation** and the difficulties experienced in forming relationships both with other individuals and within the community.

what is 'good English'?

5 Although the twentieth century brought a widening of artistic acceptance, some writers reacted to this by restricting themselves to a narrow, highly educated audience who became an academic and cultural elite. There have been a number of critics who pronounced the 'death of the novel'. This is related to novelists like T. S. Eliot, Virginia Woolf and James Joyce who consciously distanced themselves from 'popular' taste. Some writers, such as Graham Greene, made a distinction in their writing between their popular novels and their 'serious' books.

consider important historical factors

6 The 1870 Education Act made elementary education compulsory for everyone between the ages of five and thirteen. This meant that by the time of the First World War, there was a new generation of young soldiers who not only could read but were also able, for the first time in history, to write letters home describing war in all its horror. As literacy increased after the 1870 Education Act, and many more people could read and write, the effect on literature was to expand its range and to enlarge its audience, forms and subject matter.

7 The end of the Second World War did not bring any stability. The atomic age, with the dropping of bombs on Hiroshima and Nagasaki in 1945, encouraged people to think that the world might end at any moment. The war accelerated the break-up of the British Empire and forced Britain to take a careful look at its position in the world.

explore innovative structure

8 Where 'Modern' was a key word for the first part of the twentieth century, the term '**Post-Modern**' has been widely used to describe the attitudes and production of literature which followed the Second World War. Post-Modernism still concentrated on the diversity of the human condition, but the means and methods of exploring it were more varied than ever before. There were no more heroes. Instead there was the individual, solitary and lonely and responsible for his or her destiny, yet powerless against the forces of the universe. **Identity** is a common theme including sexual, local, national, racial, spiritual and intellectual.

9 Novels of the most recent years have allowed more varied voices to be heard. Those of women, racial minorities and gays have been among the voices that are clearly heard through the novel today.

✔ *Now learn how to use your knowledge*

The modern novel

Use your knowledge

1   Identify which part of the twentieth century your novel belongs and list all the characteristics and literary features of that period that it includes.

2   What were the key historical happenings of the time and what influence do you feel they had on the novel?

3   Examine the hero or heroine. How are his/her thoughts and feelings described and presented in the text? Are they conveyed successfully? Do you empathise with them?

4   How is time handled in the novel? Does the beginning of the story occur at the beginning of the novel?

5   What do you consider to be the theme of the novel? Is this consistent with the common themes of the era?

6   Do you feel that the novel could be read and understood by any reader, or are there some allusions that only a certain audience might understand?

7   How is the novel innovative in its form or use of language? Do features that are usually considered 'bad English', such as repetition of words, occur?

8   What kind of moral message do you feel is being made? Is one being made at all?

Answers on page 88

Practical criticism: prose

Test your knowledge

1 The _____ of a novel is the central idea or meaning of the story, providing a unifying point from which the plot can revolve.

2 In a novel, the _____ is the teller of the story, the voice whose point of view influences our understanding of the characters and events.

3 _____ is the way in which a text gels, the way that paragraphs in a given text fit together and follow on from one another in a logical order.

4 Tick the correct boxes to indicate whether the following words contain soft or hard consonant sounds:

    (a) jabbing   ☐ soft   ☐ hard
    (b) fluffy   ☐ soft   ☐ hard
    (c) meander   ☐ soft   ☐ hard
    (d) rock   ☐ soft   ☐ hard

5 Identify the images in the following sentences as either 'similes' or 'metaphors':

    (a) She slept on the bed like a coiled snake.
    (b) The big bear of a man towered over the crowd.
    (c) The moon glowed as if it were a rounded diamond.
    (d) The petals of snowflakes floated to the ground.

6 The left-hand column contains a list of colours. The right-hand column contains a list of associations. Connect the colours with the appropriate associations

    (a) Black   1 Nature, envy, jealousy
    (b) White   2 Anger, passion, fire, aggression
    (c) Green   3 Cold, icy, natural
    (d) Red   4 Superstition, magic, supernatural, death
    (e) Blue   5 Royalty, pomp and circumstance, supernatural
    (f) Gold   6 Innocence, purity, virginity, blankness, peace
    (g) Purple   7 Precious, expensive, elusive, gaudy

Answers

1 theme   2 narrator   3 cohesion   4 (a) hard, (b) soft, (c) soft, (d) hard   5 (a) simile, (b) metaphor, (c) simile, (d) metaphor   6 a-4, b-6, c-1, d-2, e-3, f-7, g-5

 if you got them all right, skip to page 59

Practical criticism: prose

Improve your knowledge

20 minutes

Unseen practical criticism involves writing a response to a short text that you have not previously studied. However, many of the skills that you have acquired during the study of your set texts will be helpful with unseen texts, although you will have to apply your own literary understanding rather than using ideas that you have read or been taught. You must be able to read and make sense of the text quickly, recognise its important features, understand how the writer has used language, style and structure and express your understanding of these in a logical and concise essay.

consider when the text was written

Examiners choose the prose extracts so that there are plenty of interesting features to write about. Do not panic if, on a first reading, you feel lost; the key to a sensitive response is a close re-reading, paying careful attention to the choice of vocabulary and sentence structure. It is sometimes helpful to remember that a writer's aim is to remove you from your own reality and place you in an entirely new world of his or her making. Therefore they must choose words that paint a vivid picture and literary techniques that bring this new world alive. You should ask yourself – of all the thousands of words in the English language, why has the writer chosen to use these ?

a personal response is important

read the text closely and carefully

It is helpful to have some kind of **strategy**, or **checklist of features** to look for, and the following should provide you with the basis of such a list:

1 Identify what the **core** of the text is about and in this way you will identify the **theme**. Once you have done this, try to extend your ideas by considering how this writer has made the theme individual to the text. The title of the novel or chapter can be important in influencing your interpretation of the theme.

2 Consider whose **voice** it is that tells the story. Is the voice in the first or third person, does the **narrator** have an active part in the plot, or do they merely observe? Check to see if the narrator tells you what the other characters are thinking or what they have done in the past or will do in the future.

the narrator tells the story in prose, not the author

3 The structure of the writing is important in establishing **cohesion** within the text. Usually, there are obvious ways in which the text can be divided into sections, either by its layout, its meaning or by changes in the way the language is used. Try to establish how the structure aids your understanding of the writer's handling of the theme and subject matter.

The **structure of sentences**, their length and complexity can also add to the mood of the text. Long sentences can make the atmosphere seem monotonous and slow the pace. Complicated construction can reflect complex ideas or confusion; short sentences can mirror simplicity or accelerate the pace. The use of **listing** items in a text can have several effects: it can make the description seem tedious ('I bought some groceries' compared with 'I bought some potatoes and beans and carrots and onions and parsnips and broccoli' etc.) or in a different context, it can emphasise the quantity of something ('in her handbag she had money, keys, make-up, tissues, an address book, pens, notepads – I'm surprised she didn't have the kitchen sink!'). Note here that the plurals aid the emphasis on quantity.

4 **Tone** sets the atmosphere which pervades the text (dark and depressing, bright, lively and colourful, slow and lethargic). You should try to consider what features in the writing help create this effect. Have a close look at the sentence lengths and complexity. The sounds of the words can also influence the mood – **soft consonant sounds** provide a relaxed or romantic mood and hard consonant sounds create a more tempestuous and aggressive mood.

questions often focus on use of language

5 You should examine how the writer uses **similes** and **metaphors**, what types of images are used and whether they have anything in common. For example, are all the images natural, or to do with death, or very beautiful, or religious? Try to consider what overall effect the imagery has on the description of the text.

'**Collocation**' is simply the company that words keep. Words either collocate strongly, that is, they are often used together in general English usage (blond and hair, car and exhaust) or they collocate weakly, that is, they are rarely used together (hair and exhaust, car and blond). Authors often use weak collocations in their writing because new combinations of words create new effects. Although this technique is mostly used in poetry, where the concentration of the meaning of each word is magnified, it is also used in prose, and you should take note of unusual combinations of words and consider what effect they have.

6 Make a note of the **colours** used throughout the text and the kind of picture that they paint. Are they dreary, depressing, bright, rich or natural? The connotations of the colours may add to the atmosphere, for example, black has associations with death and the supernatural, white with purity and innocence, red with passion and anger.

For a writer to convey a picture to you vividly, all five of your senses must be stimulated. You must be able to see, in your imagination, the scene described, hear the sounds, feel the temperature, taste and smell as the characters do, empathise with their emotions. It can be significant if one or more of these senses is not described; consider the effect that this has on the description – is the sound sense deliberately ignored to emphasise the silence of the scene, for example?

use the text for evidence

Now learn how to use your knowledge

Use your knowledge

1 Using the checklist, describe how Scott Fitzgerald makes the description of this scene vivid. You should consider how the author has used language and literary devices to achieve this effect.

The Great Gatsby by F. Scott Fitzgerald
Chapter III

There was music from my neighbor's house through the summer nights. In his blue gardens men and girls came and went like moths among the whisperings and the champagne and the stars. At high tide in the afternoon I watched his guests diving from the tower of his raft, or taking the sun on the hot sand of his beach while his two motor-boats slit the waters of the Sound, drawing aquaplanes over cataracts of foam. On weekends his Rolls-Royce became an omnibus, bearing parties to and from the city between nine in the morning and long past midnight, while his station wagon scampered like a brisk yellow bug to meet all trains. And on Mondays eight servants, including an extra gardener, toiled all day with mops and scrubbing-brushes and hammers and garden-shears, repairing the ravages of the night before.

Every Friday five crates of oranges and lemons arrived from a fruiterer in New York – every Monday these same oranges and lemons left his back door in a pyramid of pulpless halves. There was a machine in the kitchen which could extract the juice of two hundred oranges in half an hour if a little button was pressed two hundred times by a butler's thumb.

At least once a fortnight a corps of caterers came down with several hundred feet of canvas and enough colored lights to make a Christmas tree of Gatsby's enormous garden. On buffet tables, garnished with glistening hors-d'oeuvre, spiced baked hams crowded against salads of harlequin designs and pastry pigs and turkeys bewitched to a dark gold. In the main hall a bar with a real brass rail was set up, and stocked with gins and liquors and with cordials so long forgotten that most of his female guests were too young to know one from another.

By seven o'clock the orchestra has arrived – no thin five-piece affair, but a whole pit full of oboes and trombones and saxophones and viols and cornets and piccolos, and low and high drums. The last swimmers have come in from the beach now and are dressing upstairs; the cars from New York are parked five deep in the drive, and already the halls and salons and verandas are gaudy with primary colors and hair bobbed in strange new ways and shawls beyond the dreams of Castile. The bar is in full swing, and floating rounds of cocktails permeate the garden outside until the air is alive with chatter and laughter and casual innuendo and introductions forgotten on the spot and enthusiastic meeting between women who never knew each other's names.

The lights grow brighter as the earth lurches away from the sun, and now the orchestra is playing yellow cocktail music and the opera of voices pitches a key higher. Laughter is easier minute by minute, spilled with prodigality, tipped out at a cheerful word. The groups change more swiftly, swell with new arrivals, dissolve and form in the same breath – already there are wanderers, confident girls who weave here and there among the stouter and more stable, become for a sharp, joyous moment the center of a group and then, excited with triumph glide on through the sea-change of faces and voices and color under the constantly changing light.

Answers on page 89

Poetry toolbox 1

Test your knowledge

30 minutes

This chapter covers structure, rhythm, rhyme and tone. The next chapter focuses on imagery and language.

1 The organisation of the poem is called the _____. Poets employ a variety of forms which can be defined by looking at the structure of the _____.

2 A rhyming couplet is a _____ _____ _____ _____ and a quatrain is a stanza that has _____ lines.

3 Rhythm can be defined as the way a poem _____. This can be closely studied by looking at how the poet has arranged _____ and light syllables.

4 The term which describes the arrangement of stressed and light syllables is _____. An _____ metre is where one light syllable is followed by one stressed syllable.

5 A poet arranges the syllables into groups called _____. The term which describes a line or poetry with five groups of syllables is called a _____.

6 Rhyme can be described as the way the poet _____ the sounds of the words. There are different types of rhyme such as _____ rhyme which describes two words that do not exactly match.

7 Match the examples with the terms to describe their sound:

    (a) Consonance   (i) I grow old . . . I grow old . . .
                                  I shall wear the bottoms of my trousers rolled

    (b) Onomatopoeia   (ii) Beggars brag of burnt out boxes
    (c) Alliteration   (iii) Only the stuttering rifles' rapid rattle
    (d) Assonance   (iv) Buried beneath some snow-deep Alps.

8 Tone can be described as the _____ behind the words.

Answers

If you got them all right, skip to page 65

1 form, stanza   **2** pair of rhymed lines, four   **3** moves, stressed   **4** metre, iambic   **5** feet, pentameter   **6** organises, imperfect   **7** a iv, b iii, c ii, d i   **8** emotion or attitude

Poetry toolbox 1

Improve your knowledge

60 minutes

1 Form

The way the poet has **organised** the poem. You should always try to think about the form of the poem and how it relates to the content of the poem.

2 Varieties of forms

Stanza structure	Definition
Rhyming couplet	Pair of rhymed lines.
Tercet	Three line stanzas, single rhyme.
Quatrain	Four line stanza, abcb or abab.
Heroic quatrain	Iambic pentameter, abab.
Rime Royal	Seven line stanza, iambic pentameter ab, ab, bcc.
Octavia Rima	Eight line stanza, comic effect, ab ab ab cc.
Sonnet	Lyric, one stanza, fourteen iambic pentameter lines, intricate rhyme scheme.
Petrarchan sonnet	Octave and sestet, ab ba ab ba cde cde.
Shakespearean sonnet	Three quatrains, one couplet abab cdcd efef gg.
Spenserian sonnet	Rhyme links each quatrain to the next, abab bcbc cdcd ee.
Lyric	Short, song-like verse, conveys emotion, mood.
Ballad	Quatrain narrative, often contains a refrain.
Mock heroic	Treatment of a trivial subject.
Lament	Short poem conveys intense grief.

3   Rhythm

The study of the **movement** of the poem which is defined by the organisation of **stressed** and **light syllables**.

Term	Definition	Example	Effect
Iambic	One light one stressed	That time of year thou mayst in me behold	Thoughtful, uncertainty to certainty.
Anapaestic	Two light one stressed	When I went to the bar	Builds tension.
Trochaic	One stressed one light	Lay your sleeping head, my love	Assertive.
Dactylic	One stressed two light	Woman much missed, how you call to me . . .	Sadness/loss.
Spondaic	Two stressed	All whom war, death age	Bold.

4   The length of the line is described as the number of **feet** it contains. A foot is a unit of syllables.

5   There are technical terms for a line with a specific number of feet. These are:

- monometer – one foot
- dimeter – two feet
- trimeter – three feet
- tetrameter – four feet
- pentameter – five feet
- hexameter – six feet
- heptameter – seven feet
- octameter – eight feet.

6   Rhyme

The way the poet arranges the sounds of the words.

Internal rhyme

The day she visited the dissecting room — Masculine
They had four men laid out, black as burnt turkey — rhyme
Already half unstrung. A vinegary fume
Of the death vats clung to them: — Imperfect rhyme
The white-smocked boys started working.
The head of his cadaver had caved in, — Feminine
And she could scarcely make out anything — end rhyme
In that rubble of skull plates and old leather. — Perfect
A sallow piece of string held it together. — end rhyme

Sylvia Plath *Two Views of a Cadaver Room*

- End rhyme – last stressed syllable of the line rhymes.
- Internal rhyme – words that rhyme within the line.
- Masculine rhyme – words with one syllable (**monosyllabic**).
- Feminine rhyme – words with two syllables (**polysyllabic**).
- Perfect rhyme – words rhyme exactly.
- Imperfect rhyme – partial, near rhyme.

7 Sound

A poet will often deliberately choose a word to **echo the meaning**. The technical terms to describe sounds are:

- alliteration – repetition of similar sounds (contributes to tone)
- assonance – repetition of vowel sounds
- consonance – repetition of same consonants but different vowel sounds
- onomatopoeia – sound echoes the sense (contributes to atmosphere).

8 Tone

Rhythm and rhyme contribute to the **tone** of the poem. Think about tone as the **emotion** or **attitude** behind the words. The tone of a poem can be:

- conventional
- dense
- bold
- grave
- familiar
- clear
- reserved
- whimsical

Study the following verse which is annotated to explain further rhythm and metre.

1 foot

Rhythm = syllables	Womăn mŭch	míssed, hŏw yŏu	cáll tŏ mĕ,	cáll tŏ mĕ,	*4 feet = tetrameter*
1 stressed	Saýĭng thăt	noŭ yŏu arĕ	nót aš yŏu	wére	*3 feet = trimeter*
and 2 light	Whén yŏu hăd	changed frŏm thĕ	one whŏ wăs	áll tŏ mĕ,	*4 feet = tetrameter*
(⁀⁀) *= dactyl*	Bút aš ăt	fírst whĕn oŭr	dáy wăs fãir.		*3 feet = trimeter*

Form: Four lines per stanza

Poetry toolbox 1

Use your knowledge

45 minutes

The Voice

Woman much missed, how you call to me, call to me,
Saying that now you are not as you were
When you had changed from the one who was all to me,
But as at first when our day was fair.

Can it be you that I hear? Let me view you, then,
Standing as when I drew near to the town
Where you would wait for me: yes, as I knew you then,
Even to the original air-blue gown!

Or is it only the breeze, in its listlessness
Travelling across the wet mead to me here,
You being ever dissolved to wan wistlessness,
Heard no more again far or near?

Thus I; faltering forward,
Leaves around me falling,
Wind oozing thin through the thorn from norward,
And the woman calling.

Thomas Hardy (*December 1912*)

1 The form of the stanza is called a _____ which is commonly used in _____.

2 The pattern of syllables in line one has _____ stressed syllable followed by _____ light syllables. This is called a _____.

3 Lines one and three have _____ feet in a line which is called a _____. Lines two and four have _____ feet which is called a _____.

65

4 The rhyme scheme of the poem is described as _____. This is regular throughout the poem, in which the most prominent sound is of the _____.

5 The pauses in lines seven and thirteen are called _____. The interruption of the rhythm has the effect of _____.

6 Lines _____ have feminine endings and lines _____ have masculine endings. The masculine end-rhymes represent _____ whereas the feminine endings reflect _____.

7 The poem is mostly in _____ rhyme although _____ is an example of internal rhyme in the poem.

✓ *Answers on page 90*

Poetry toolbox 2

Test your knowledge

30 minutes

1 The function of imagery is to add to and _____ the meaning of the poem.

2 Poets often convey imagery through the use of figurative language which includes:

- metaphor which is _____ _____ _____ _____ _____
- simile which is _____ _____ _____ _____ _____
- symbol which _____ _____ _____ _____ _____.

3 Contrasting images creates _____ and focuses attention on the conflict between the images. Images can also be _____ for emphasis, or they can be _____ when they refer to knowledge outside of the text, or created through word association which is described as _____.

4 Poets can create effective images through the use of the senses. The words to explain this are

_____ – images you can hear
_____ – images you can touch
_____ – images you can smell
_____ – images you can taste
_____ – images you can see
_____ – images describing movement
_____ – images describing temperature.

5 An examiner is interested in my opinions about the poet as long as it is _____ to the question and _____ by textual evidence. I also need to show an appreciation of the _____ of the poem.

If you got them all right, skip to page 71

Poetry toolbox 2

Improve your knowledge

60 minutes

1. **Imagery** creates mental pictures; C. S. Lewis described imagery as 'a picture made out of words'. When you read a poem, allow yourself to experience the words one by one and then put them together. You will then be able to analyse the poet's choice of words and how they are **combined** to produce an **overall effect**. The choice of images will suggest something about the meaning of the poem.

2. Poets have to use words **economically** and therefore will convey meaning in a condensed way. An efficient and effective device to convey meaning is through **comparison**.

   Metaphors and **similes** are both employed to make the reader think about comparing one thing to another; a metaphor is a direct comparison, e.g. 'Jack was a lion', whereas a simile is a indirect comparison, e.g. 'Jack was as angry as a lion.' A useful way to explain a metaphor is to use the terms **tenor** and **vehicle**.

   similes will have 'like' or 'as' in the phrase

   - The tenor is the subject being compared – Jack
   - The vehicle is what the subject is being compared to – the lion.

   You could then explain the metaphor like this:

   The vehicle (the lion) in the above metaphor is effective as it conveys the anger and the power of the tenor (Jack).

   A **symbol** is also an efficient way to convey meaning because it represents rather than describes in detail. For example 'A broken heart' is not really a broken heart but representative of failed love and sorrow.

   always say why the symbol, simile or metaphor is effective

3 Poets use a variety of techniques to make imagery effective. Look at the following lines of poetry and note the different uses of images.

- **contrasted** – 'Soft, feathery fingertips foraged and forced'
  This builds tension between the tactile image of the fingertips and the violent images of the actions 'foraged' and 'forced'.

- **repeated** –   With blackest moss the flower-pots
                        Were thickly crusted, one and all:
                     The rusted nails fell from the knots
                        That held the pear to the gable-wall.
                     The broken sheds look'd sad and strange:
                        Unlifted was the clinking latch:
                        Weeded and worn the ancient thatch
                     Upon the lonely moated grange.
                        Mariana Alfred Lord Tennyson

  Tennyson repeats images of decay, deterioration and wildness. This state of degeneration is a metaphor for Mariana herself.

- **allusions** – 'The Chair she sat in, like a burnished throne,'
  is a line from T. S. Eliot's second part to *The Waste Land* and alludes to Enobarbus' description of Cleopatra in Shakespeare's *Antony and Cleopatra*. Eliot utilises the idea of the beautiful female's mythic status and then undermines it with his description of modern women who make such banal statements as 'My nerves are bad tonight.'

  look up any allusions in Brewer's Phrase and Fable or a dictionary

- **word association** –
                     'The dawn, the dawn,' and died away;
                     And East and West, without a breath,
                     Mixt their dim lights, like life and death,
                     To broaden into boundless day.'
                        XCV *In Memoriam A. H. H.*
                        Alfred Lord Tennyson

  Tennyson uses time (dawn) and the idea that the directions, East and West, convey a change in state. The reader is encouraged to think that the change in state is on a universal scale by using such universal images whereas it is actually a response to the death of his friend Hallam and the awareness that life continues regardless and eternally.

4 **Concrete imagery** is imagery which appeals to the senses rather than being figurative. Poets employ concrete imagery to make an immediate and vivid impact which provokes a reaction. Look at the following definitions and examples:

Term	Definition	Example
Auditory	Hear	That muted boom, that clangor Sylvia Plath *Nightshift*
Tactile	Touch	Your temples, where the hair crowded in, Were the tender place. Ted Hughes *The Tender Place*
Olfactory	Smell	The winter evening settles down With smell of steaks in passageways. T. S. Eliot *Preludes*
Gustatory	Taste	Black sweet blood mouthfuls, Sylvia Plath *Ariel*
Visual	See	Webster was much possessed by death And saw the skull beneath the skin; And breastless creatures under ground Leaned backward with a lipless grin. T. S. Eliot *Whispers of Immortality*
Kinaesthetic	Movement	When we had given our bodies to the wind And all the shadowy banks on either side Came sweeping through the darkness, spinning still The rapid line of motion, then at once Have I, reclining back upon my heels, Stopped short; yet still the solitary cliffs Wheeled by me . . . William Wordsworth *Preludes*
Thermal	Hot/cold	Little poppies, little hell flames, Sylvia Plath *Poppies in July*

 Examiners **are** interested in your response and personal interpretation of a poem **but** you must be able to support your opinion with textual evidence. Look at the following comments about the poem by T. S. Eliot which is used as the example for visual imagery above.

I think T.S. Eliot's poem is a macabre poem and is very negative.

Although this comment is accurate, it does not explain how the student arrived at this view. The following comment is better:

The macabre mood of the poem is achieved through the images of 'skull beneath the skin' and 'breastless creatures under ground'. By opening the poem with such surreal images, Eliot forces the reader to be as 'possessed by death' as Webster is.

Poetry toolbox 2

Use your knowledge

45 minutes

1 Read the following extract from Christina Rossetti's *Goblin Market,* a narrative poem about two sisters, one of whom (Laura) buys and eats the forbidden, cursed fruit from the Goblin Men. Annotate the poem according to:

(1) metaphors
(2) similes,
(3) imagery,
(4) symbols,
(5) allusions,
(6) word association,

(7) tactile imagery,
(8) visual imagery,
(9) thermal imagery,
(10) gustatory imagery,
(11) repeated images.

> I ate and ate my fill,
> Yet my mouth waters still;
> To-morrow night I will buy more: and kissed her:
> 'Have done with sorrow;
> I'll bring you plums to-morrow
> Fresh on their mother twigs,
> Cherries worth getting;
> You cannot think what fits
> My teeth have met in,
> What melons ice-cold
> Piled on a dish of gold
> Too huge for me to hold,
> What peaches with a velvet nap,
> Pellucid grapes without one seed:
> Odorous indeed must be the mead
> Whereon they grow, and pure the wave they drink
> With lilies at the brink,
> And sugar-sweet their sap.'

Golden head by golden head,
Like two pigeons in one nest
Folded in each other's wings,
They lay down in their curtained bed:
Like two blossoms on one stem
Like two flakes of new-fall'n snow,
Like two wands of ivory
Tipped with gold for awful kings.
Moon and stars gazed in at them,
Wind sang to them lullaby,
Lumbering owls forbore to fly,
Not a bat flapped to and fro
Round their nest:
Cheek to cheek and breast to breast
Locked together in one nest.

Answers on page 91

Chaucer

15 minutes

Test your knowledge

1   Chaucer was writing in the _____ century.

2   Chaucer wrote *The Canterbury Tales* which are a collection of _____.

3   The narrative voice who occasionally intervenes is the _____. He is important because _____.

4   Five characters from *The Canterbury Tales* are:

   _____
   _____
   _____
   _____
   _____

5   In my study of Chaucer I should note how the character's _____ relates to the _____ they tell.

6   *The Canterbury Tales* consists mainly of _____ pentameter lines and _____ couplets.

7   I should always use quotations from an edition which uses _____ English rather than Modern English.

8   I need to show the examiners my understanding of the _____ devices employed, the _____ delineation and Chaucer's narrative skills.

Answers

1 fourteenth   2 prologues and tales told by various characters from differing social classes to win a competition for the best tale set by their host (Chaucer)   3 host, he provides the framework for the tales, adding realism and purpose for the narratives that follow   4 for a full list of characters see *Improve your knowledge*, page 74   5 prologue, tale   6 iambic, heroic   7 middle   8 poetic, character

 If you got them all right, skip to page 79

Chaucer

Improve your knowledge

60 minutes

1 Chaucer's life

Chaucer was born between 1340 and 1345 and died in 1400. During this period major events such as The Hundred Years War, The Black Death, The Peasants' Revolt and the deposition of Richard II occurred. Chaucer was writing in a time of great change, not only historically but also in terms of the progress of the English language. French was the language of the court and English was seen as common. Chaucer's decision to write in his vernacular, English (we call it Middle English), was revolutionary. He was taught in French and most literature would have been either in Latin or French. Chaucer was so popular in his time and contributed so much to English Literature that John Dryden called him the 'father of English poetry'. Chaucer was interested in all forms of living and experienced life to the full. Interests such as:

- the relationship between the natural world and the human world
- how life was organised in terms of hierarchies
- the exploration and effect of the social class system

are evident in the diverse range of characters and situations he represents in *The Canterbury Tales*.

2 The Canterbury Tales

The Canterbury Tales is much shorter than Chaucer originally intended it to be when he started it in 1387. We cannot be certain of the correct order of the tales. The situation as described in *The General Prologue* is that a band of travellers to Canterbury meets in a public house in London. The host invites them all to tell a tale and offers a prize for the best tale. The band of travellers includes:

Genteel class:	Knight and son
	Squire and attendant Yeomen
Church representatives:	Prioress and Nun, personal Chaplain
	Monk
	Friar

Others:	Merchant
	Oxford Clerk, Sergeant of the Law
	Franklin
	Guildsman and Tradesman
	Widow: Wife of Bath
	Parson, Reeve
	Miller
	Summoner
	Pardoner

You are not expected to know all of these characters, but you should be aware that Chaucer is able to write from a multiplicity of viewpoints successfully and skilfully.

Narrative voice

The overall persona is the host who describes himself in *The General Prologue* as a portly, bookish, well-meaning, dim-witted man, who may not entertain his audience to their satisfaction. Notice how the host undermines his own ability; the effect is that when the audience (us) has heard the tales, we will be more pleased because they are better than expected. By using a **persona** like the host to convey the tales to the audience, Chaucer the poet, distances himself from the opinions expressed by the various characters and cannot therefore be blamed for any unconventional or unpopular views.

Look for the following distinctive features in the narrative voice telling the tale.

- Tone – satirical, plaintive, accusatory, humorous
- Rhythm – heroic couplets to represent units of meaning
- Imagery – use of commercial, religious, sexual images
- Mood – sorrowful, regretful, anxious, judgemental
- Structure – monologues, interruptions.

One key thing to remember is that even though you may be studying *The Miller's Tale* for example, it is Chaucer who **controls the narrative**. There will be conflicts between speakers and their ideas; again remember Chaucer is the puppet master and it is he who manipulates your point of view although the opinions the characters express are not necessarily his own.

Characters

These are numerous and diverse. Chaucer manipulates our views of the characters by **exaggerating** one particular characteristic or aspect to their personality. This means that the characterisation is almost a **caricature**. Look at this (modernised) extract of the description of the Wife of Bath from *The General Prologue*:

gap toothed =
high sex drive
to Chaucer's
audience

> For she was gap-toothed, if you take my meaning.
> Comfortably on an ambling horse she sat,
> Well-wimpled, wearing on her head a hat
>   That might have been a shield in size and shape
> A riding-skirt round her enormous hips,
> Also a pair of sharp spurs on her feet.
> In company, how she could laugh and joke!
> No doubt she knew all the cures for love,
> For at that game she was a past mistress.

Notice the exaggerated trait here is on the vastness of the wife, physically and in terms of personality and sexuality.

Relationship between character and tale

Avoid considering the character's prologue as distinct from the tale they tell. Try to keep in mind the purpose of *The Canterbury Tales* – to win a competition for telling the best story. Whatever you learn about the character, always consider whether the tale they tell is appropriate.

Style

When you are writing about Chaucer's style, keep firmly in mind that you are analysing the language and everything you have revised in *Poetry Toolbox 1* and *2* is still very much relevant. The following features are particularly applicable to Chaucer:

remember
The Canterbury
Tales was
intended to be
read aloud to a
live audience!

- **intimate conversational undertone;**
    'But yet I praye to all this **compaignye**   (company)
    If that I speke after my fantyse
    For mine **entente** nis but for to **pleye**.   (intent, play)
    Now, sire, now wol I tell you forth my tale.'
- **rhetorical questions:**
    'Wher can ye seye, in any manere age,
    That heighe God **defended** mariage   (condemned)
    By expres word? I pray you, telleth me.
    Or where he comanded virginitee?'

- **description**

'Her **coverchiefs** ful fine weren of ground-	(head scarf)
I dorste swere they **weyeden** ten pound-	(weighed)
That on a Sunday weren upon her head.	
Her **hosen** weren of fin scarlet red,	(hosiery)
Ful **streite yteyd,** and shoes ful moiste and newe.	(tightly laced)
Boold was her face, and fair, and reed of **hewe**.'	(hue)

Rhythm: Iambic pentameter

Chaucer was the first poet to use the way the French wrote poetry (French versification) within the boundaries of his language, what we now call Middle English. Chaucer was the first poet to use the **rhyming pentameter** also known as the **heroic couplet**. This is the principal meter for *The Canterbury Tales.*

look this up in Poetry Toolbox 1 if you don't remember

7 Middle English

So called because it comes between Old English (e.g. Beowulf) and Modern English. You should try reading Chaucer's poetry aloud because it is only then that you develop a sense of his rhythmical skill and note how effective it is as a storytelling medium. Chaucer's poetry was listened to rather than read as printing presses did not exist. Remember the following points about Middle English to help your reading:

- sounds are often similar to Modern English
- unfamiliar words and references are usually explained in footnotes
- some words may be familiar but the meanings will have changed (e.g. 'defended' in Middle English means 'condemned' but today means 'protected')
- the syntax (order of words) may not be familiar – try to establish why Chaucer has ordered the words in that way
- listen to a tape recording either from your school, local library or book shop.

Words that occur frequently are well worth remembering. These are:

er = before	eek/eke = and/also
hir = their	siker = sure

don't forget to use the glossary at the back of your Chaucer text

When reading aloud try to remember how personal pronouns are pronounced. This will help you to appreciate the rhythm of the lines.

he = hay	I = ee
she = shay	my = mee
me = may	mine = meen
they = thy-ee	

Remember Chaucer's:

- **narrative skill** – the stories are amusing and entertaining; consider how appropriate the story is to the character
- **narrative voice** – Chaucer uses personas to convey the Prologues and Tales but always remember that it is Chaucer who is the puppeteer
- **character delineation:** one aspect of the character is usually exaggerated; this is effective because it allows the audience to appreciate their personality in a relatively short amount of text
- **poetic devices** – analyse the text closely for the features of speech, imagery, metaphors and similes.

read the character description in The General Prologue – remember TRIMS!

Now learn how to use your knowledge

Chaucer

Use your knowledge

1 Chaucer was interested in _____ and this is demonstrated in the _____ through _____ and plot.

2 The *Prologue* and the *Tale* I am studying explores the theme of _____.

3 The three distinctive stylistic features of the speaker in the prologue and tale I am studying are _____ , _____ , and _____.

4 The character I am studying has the following four features: _____ , _____ , _____ and _____.

5 The character's prologue is an appropriate match to their tale because _____.

6 The use of the heroic couplet in the tale I am studying conveys _____.

7 In order to fully appreciate the rhythms and metre of the prologue and tale I must attempt to _____.

✔ *Answers on page 91*

Practical criticism: poetry

10 minutes

1 The _____ of a poem is found above the text and can give an indication of the subject matter and poet's opinions.

2 There are two types of imagery. One is a _____ and the other is a _____.

3 Which linguistic term identifies 'the company that words keep'?

4 What word would you use to describe the associations that we have with particular words?

5 What is Phonology the study of?

6 When an inanimate object is given human attributes, it is called _____.

7 The _____ of a poem can identify parallel grammar or themes in the stanzas.

8 The _____ of lines and their _____ can mirror the content or events in the poem.

9 The _____ of a poem is created by the natural stresses placed on syllables in words in a line of poetry.

Answers

If you got them all right, skip to page 83

Practical criticism: poetry

Improve your knowledge

45 minutes

A poet's aim is to communicate his or her insight into worldly experience, sharing that experience with the reader. To achieve this, the poet must use language which does not just rely on the reader's understanding of the dictionary definition, but on their intellect, memory, senses and the readers' associations with those words. As with analysing unseen prose, it is helpful to have a checklist of literary devices to be aware of.

don't make statements of fact about a poem, when they're your opinions or speculation

1 Title
The **title** of the poem will be an important key to your understanding of the poem. It should give you an indication of the **theme** of the poem, but may also hint at the poet's opinion or identify a second meaning in the poem. Think carefully about the words used, their meaning and why the poet has chosen to use them. It is also helpful to summarise briefly what ideas you feel that the poet is trying to communicate.

write about impressions or feelings you get from the poetry

2 Imagery
Used to great extent and effect in poetry and you will need to be able to identify **similes** and **metaphors**. You should think carefully about the image used and why the poet has included such a picture. Think of the qualities that the picture has. Often you will find that poets use 'extended' metaphors, which simply means that the same image or picture is used throughout the poem. For example, describing the sea as if it behaved like a vicious dog could be the start of an extended metaphor.

3 Collocation
Because poetry uses relatively few words to express ideas, the **company** that those words keep will directly affect their meaning. Therefore, an examination of **collocation** within the poem is important.

Connotation

Always be aware of the **connotations** of the words used in the poem. A dictionary will provide the definition of what a word means, but poetry relies on the connotations that we have with certain words, that is, the **associations** that we hold with words and what they mean to us as part of a social group.

make sure that you always mention the contribution to the poem as a whole of the various techniques used

Phonology

The **sounds of the words** in the poem can reflect the sounds made by what is being described. The most obvious way of achieving this is through **onomatopoeia**, but **alliteration** can also be used. This provides another sense perception and can bring the portrayal alive audibly.

Personification

When poets attribute human qualities to an inanimate object, the object is 'personified'. If **personification** is used in a poem, consider what effect the poet is attempting to achieve and why.

Structure

It is important to identify the **structure** of the poem. It may be useful to re-read *Poetry Toolbox 1* at this stage, but you should also summarise the content of each stanza to identify any parallel themes or grammatical structures. Sometimes questions are asked; if so, how are the answers handled? Are we left to answer the question, or does the poet provide the response?

Number and length of lines

You should take a close look at **line length** and **number** of lines per stanza. This can mirror the poet's attitude towards the subject matter or theme. You may find that the climax of a poem is portrayed by a break in the regularity of the line length, or by an uneven number of lines in a stanza. The ear does not want to hear irregularity, and therefore a sense of unease can be created.

don't call stanzas or verses 'chapters' don't call the poet 'the author' don't call the poem 'the book'!

Rhythm

Rhythm and rhyme can be used in much the same way. Consistent rhyme schemes and lilting rhythm create a musical balance. A break in this tends to mirror a break in the tranquillity of the content of the poem. Half rhymes are often used to this effect

Now learn how to use your knowledge

Practical criticism: poetry

60 minutes

Use your knowledge

1   Read the following poem carefully. How does Owen portray the plight of the soldiers effectively?

> **Anthem for Doomed Youth**
>
> What passing-bells for those who die as cattle?
>   Only the monstrous anger of the guns.
> Only the stuttering rifles' rapid rattle
>   Can patter out their hasty orisons.
> No mockeries now for them: no prayers nor bells,
> Nor any voice of mourning save the choirs, –
> The shrill, demented choirs of wailing shells;
> And bugles calling for them from sad shires.
>
> What candles may be held to speed them all?
> Not in the hands of boys, but in their eyes
>   Shall shine the holy glimmers of good-byes.
> The pallor of girls' brows shall be their pall;
>   Their flowers the tenderness of patient minds,
>   And each slow dusk a drawing-down of blinds.
>
>   Wilfred Owen

✔ *Answers on page 92*

Answers to

Use your knowledge tests

Revision and exam technique: essay writing

'As the sole evil character in *Snow-White*, the step-mother is fully culpable for Snow-White's near demise.' How far do you agree with this statement?

1 Analyse the key words in the question:

- sole – single, only, one
- evil – corrupt, immoral with no feeling of guilt or conscience
- fully – absolutely, totally
- culpable – to blame, at fault, responsible for
- demise – death, fatality.

2 Re-word the question: the step-mother is the only really corrupt and immoral character in the story and Snow-White's near death is completely her fault. The question assumes that the other characters do no evil and do not hold any responsibility for her near fatality.

3 Make an essay plan:

Agree	Disagree
The Queen is obsessed by her own beauty – vain to the point of obsession.	The king marries very soon after his first wife's death and seems to do nothing to protect Snow-White.
She thinks nothing of murder, and readily involves the huntsman in her evil plans.	Although the huntsman lets Snow-White go, he knows that she could be eaten by the animals, so he is at fault too.
Her three attempts and final success at murdering Snow-White are premeditated; they are carefully planned and executed.	The dwarfs realise Snow-White's danger, but still leave her alone all day – even after she has nearly been murdered twice. Snow-White disobeys the dwarfs' instructions, because she cannot resist temptation – therefore she should take some of the blame.

4 Write an introduction which gives your examiner an idea of your essay plan:

Certainly the step-mother does try to murder Snow-White, and this is evil, but the other characters, the King, the huntsman, the dwarfs and even Snow-White herself, are also partly to blame because their actions, whilst not essentially 'evil', are certainly not moral.

By naming the characters that you intend to discuss, you have indicated to the examiner the structure of your essay plan.

5   Use the three step process:

- Although the huntsman does not murder Snow-White as instructed by the Queen, he does know that in releasing her in to the forest, she will be killed and eaten by the animals
- 'he let her go, knowing that the wild beasts in the forest would no doubt devour her that night anyway'
- although superficially the huntsman's actions seem to be kind, his knowing that Snow-White will die in the forest makes his behaviour cowardly and evil. Therefore, the step-mother is not the only character to behave immorally, since, as far as the huntsman is concerned, Snow-White will die in the forest and the step-mother will never know that he has been disobedient.

6   Write a conclusion:

It would not be true to state that the step-mother is the only evil character, since the King does little to protect Snow-White, the huntsman only releases her knowing that she will be eaten by the wild animals, the dwarfs do little to protect her, even when they know that she is under threat, and Snow-White herself is disobedient and allows herself to be tempted by her appetite for pretty things and food. In this way, although the step-mother commits the murder, the other characters also play a key role in Snow-White's near demise.

Revision and exam technique: style toolbox

1   Try not to use personal pronouns – my feelings, I feel, I did, I really.

2   Make sure that you spell the characters' names correctly. Note the variety of spellings in the essay – Heathcliffe, Heathclif, Heathcliff.

3   Avoid abbreviations – doesn't, she's, can't.

4   Watch for colloquial vocabulary or slang terms – care much for, turning up, thing, makes me feel sick, a bit, to let go, doing this, he reckoned, something, Cathy has gone and all he wants to do is see her again.

5   Try to write about the text in the present tense – tries to write, Brontë shows.

6   Be careful to identify your writer correctly – 'the poet' is incorrect.

7   Use linguistic pointers appropriately – 'Having said this' could have been replaced with 'however' and 'therefore' is incorrectly used because what follows is not a conclusion from the previous sentence.

8   Try to avoid over-using particular words – description/descriptive, desperate/desperation, achieved/achieve.

Revision and exam technique: preparing your text

Many A-level students worry that they do not possess the depth of thought to be able to analyse their texts in an interesting way. The old 'I don't know how to think deeply' phrase often crops up! There are some important points:

- Every student is capable of considering their text thoughtfully; you must allow yourself the confidence to know that your own ideas are worthwhile.
- Analysing a text independently takes time. You will have to allocate a few hours to just thinking about the essence of your text. It may help to try to be objective, to explain the text in your own words to a third person.
- Be active in class discussion. It will help you to identify your own ideas, to stimulate your thought processes and provide you with counter arguments.
- Do not be afraid to push your ideas as far as possible. Always ask yourself 'why do I think this?' or 'and so, what does this mean?'

This chapter should give you some useful guidelines on preparing your text, but, by all means, develop strategies that work for you:

- Try writing key points about characters or themes with appropriate quotes on individual cards that can then be arranged in multiples of different orders.
- You may wish to link your ideas in a flow or spider diagram.
- Ideas can be effectively compared in a table.

Drama toolbox

1 Consider what the main aim of the play is.

2 Refer back to the table on pages 18 and 19. Think about what features from that period are evident in the play you are studying.

3 Remind yourself of the definitions of the terms and reflect on the most appropriate moment in the play to fit the definition.

4 Always look for evidence for your comments rather than making opinions based without evidence. A frequent mistake by even the best candidates is lack of textual evidence in their essays to support their opinions.

5 Students who concentrate on analysing the language distinguish themselves from those who just relate the plot. This can make the difference between a grade D and a B. Ensure you annotate your text and identify the key speeches for each of the main characters.

Shakespeare

1 Remind yourself of the definitions of the genres on page 26. The most important thing is to think about the way the definition fits the play you are studying.

2 It is vital to support your opinions of the characters with evidence from the text. The more evidence you collate for each character, the more analytical comments you can make.

3 Recall the comments on the extract from *King Lear*. Your summary should be similar in style, analysing and commenting on the effects produced.

4   Revise the significant actions of the main characters by thinking about what actions direct the movement of the plot.

5   If you are able to appreciate the staging of the play it shows the examiner you understand the text as a piece of drama. Always remember the play was written to be performed.

Modern drama

1   Consider how the construction of plot, creation of characters or stage directions are unconventional. The theme of the play may be particularly relevant to a twentieth-century event.

2   Moved, to sympathise with the main character, disconcerted, disturbed. These are all possible options, just remember to comment on how the dramatist produces this effect.

3   Choose from: flashback, dramatic irony, time shifts, circular plot, chaos which is resolved.

4   Think about the importance of FRAISER analysis along with the circumstances the dramatist puts them in, the characterisation they are given and what eventually happens to them.

5   Remind yourself of the comments in *Improve your knowledge*, p. 35. Your comments should be as detailed and specific.

6   (a) description of the action (b) analysis of the action (c) effect of the action.

7   Consider what the stage directions tell you about how the play should be presented to the audience. Think about how these features relate to the plot or the characters.

Prose toolbox

The answers to these questions will be different for every novel written. If you experienced problems in identifying the answers to some of the questions, you may like to consider the following:

- Reading literary critics and critical essays on your set novel will help you discover some of the answers, although knowing the text well yourself is the final solution.
- Although you must be accurate about the facts and details of the novel, there are no right or wrong opinions on the novel. A good essay will be one that argues convincingly and is well supported by evidence from the text. Try to make sure that you can justify your ideas and that they follow a logical progression.
- Be sure that you fully understand the terminology associated with writing about novels. You do not need to use advanced or complicated vocabulary, but you should take care to be accurate.
- Do not waste time in essays reminding either yourself or the examiner what happens in the plot. You should also avoid quoting lengthy passages from the novel. Both of these waste precious exam time and gain you no extra marks.

Nineteenth-century novel

This is an example of some of the comments you could have made. You should be able to identify the features and comment on the effect they produce.

2 begins with setting the scene

4 ignorant of situation

4 deprived

Jo sweeps his crossing all day long, unconscious of the link, if any link there be. He sums up his mental condition, when asked a question, by replying that he 'don't know nothink.' He knows that it's hard to keep the mud off the crossing in dirty weather, and harder still to live by doing it. Nobody taught him, even that much; he found it out.

5 impersonal narrative voice

1 condition of children

3 injustice, homelessness

6 diseased and degenerate

3 class division

Jo lives – that is to say, Jo has not yet died – in a ruinous place, known to the like of him by the name of Tom-all-Alone's. It is a black, dilapidated street, avoided by all decent people; where the crazy houses were seized upon, when their decay was far advanced, by some bold vagrants, who, after establishing their own possession, took to letting them out in lodgings. Now, these tumbling tenements contain, by night, a swarm of misery. As on the ruined human wretch, vermin parasites appear, so, these ruined shelters have bred a crowd of foul existence that crawls in and out of gaps in walls and boards; and coils itself to sleep, in maggot numbers, where the rain drips in and comes and goes, fetching and carrying fever, and sowing more evil in its every footprint than Lord Coodle and Sir Thomas Doodle and the Duke of Foodle, and all the fine gentlemen in the office, down to Zoodle, shall set right in five hundred years – though born expressly to do it.

6 poverty

3 class division

3 social welfare

7 political apathy

2 ends with cause for Jo's situation

Bleak House Charles Dickens (1853)

The modern novel

Every novel is unique and because of the enormous range of styles and acceptance of innovative form in the twentieth century, the answers to these questions will be different for every novel.

Some students find analysing the modern novel difficult, especially since by the nature of its nearness, there is little literary criticism to be read. This means that you must have confidence in your **own** ideas and use your **own** knowledge of what is, and has been, going on around you to make your own judgements.

Your relationship with the characters should be close – they are the mirror of society yesterday and today and therefore your affinity with them is important.

The themes of the novel may well relate to the concerns that you have in life, or depict the concerns of your parents or grandparents in past years.

The language will possibly reflect language use today – the acceptance of slang and dialectal forms and the rejection of 'standard English' as the only 'correct' form of English.

The content may emphasise the progress made in embracing people from other cultures, religions, sexualities and classes.

The modern novel is what the reader wishes to make of it. Your interpretation is modern literary criticism!

Practical criticism: prose

1   The text concerns the excesses and over-indulgence of a party, emphasising the shallowness and superficiality of the attending guests as they become progressively drunk. Gatsby, the host, does not seem to be in attendance, and in not being at his own debauched party, the writer perhaps alludes to the 'greatness' which accompanies his name in the title of the novel; he is not interested in this triviality and indulgence.

The excesses of the party are emphasised by the constant repetition of quantities – five crates, two hundred, a corps, several hundred feet, eight servants, a pit full, and the use of plurals – boats, mops, hams, gins, verandas.

2   The narrator is first person; he refers to 'my neighbor's house' as he observes the party from his own house next door. He has not been invited and we are immediately made aware that the description is given from his own perspective and is therefore biased. In describing the actions of the guests, he subtly condemns them for their attraction to wealth and their appetite for food, alcohol and casual relationships.

3   The narrative begins with a generalised description of the parties in the first two paragraphs, emphasising the enormous amount of preparations involved behind the scenes. In the fourth paragraph, the focus changes to the details of one party, vividly describing the food, the guests and their behaviour. The sense of immediacy and feeling that we are actually at the party ourselves is indicated by the change of tense ('has arrived') and the repetition of 'now'.

Listing is used extensively to emphasise the sheer amount of work involved with the party, its excesses of food and alcohol and Gatsby's extreme wealth. The repetition of 'and' within the listing and the starting of sentences with 'And' accentuates this 'mops and scrubbing brushes and hammers and garden shears'.

4   The tone of the prose changes through the extract. At the beginning, the tone is romantic and slow-paced 'the whisperings and the champagne and the stars'. As the narrative focuses on one particular party, the tone changes to reflect the excitement and drunkenness of the guests, quickening the pace and concentrating on the excesses in food, noise and alcohol.

5   There are similes and metaphors in the extract. Insect imagery is used to describe the guests and Gatsby's wagon fetching them from the station. The 'men and girls came and went like moths' implies that the guests are not only shallow and superficial, but that, like moths, they are attracted to the light of the party, which possibly symbolises Gatsby himself. The image of the brisk yellow bug extends the insect imagery and emphasises the idea that Gatsby's wagon is always off to pick up new guests. In the latter part of the extract, Scott Fitzgerald uses an extended metaphor of water imagery to describe the party. The narrator describes the 'floating rounds of cocktails' as the waiter transports the tray of drinks above the heads of the guests as if the guests make up an anonymous sea of drunken movement. This idea is further explored in the description of the guests' behaviour, the 'sea-change' of faces, how their conversation is 'spilled out with prodigality', 'tipped out' as it 'swells' and 'dissolves'. This water imagery emphasises the

lack of substance associated with the guests, as if they are nothing on their own, but together making up a volume of meaningless liquid.

There is use of weak collocation within the extract. The gardens are described as 'blue' to describe the garden in the night light. The cocktail music is described as yellow. Here the senses are becoming mixed – the adjective describes sight, not sound and this could reflect the confusion of the guests' senses as they become more drunk.

6   There is continual use of colour throughout the extract. The party is described in terms of 'gaudy' primary colours, blue and yellow and Christmas tree lights. The colours are bright and yellow, in particular, is often mentioned. This colour is extended into dark gold and brass, which possibly indicates that underneath the garish colours of the party hides Gatsby himself, symbolised by a more precious and valuable colour and the light which is continually repeated.

The first sense that is described is sound, the music from the Gatsby's summer parties, as if this is what first arrested the narrator's attention as he observes from next door. Time becomes an important sense as the extract progresses. The 'summer nights' are reduced to specific times of the day as the preparations are described 'afternoon', 'weekends', 'nine in the morning', 'long past midnight'. The mention of time becomes even more specific 'every Friday' and 'at least once a fortnight' until eventually with the description of this specific party, time becomes closer and faster – 'by seven o'clock' to 'minute by minute'. This brings alive the description of the party and how fast time passes for the drunken crowd.

Poetry toolbox 1

1   quatrain, ballads

2   one, two, dactyl

3   four, tetrameter, three, trimeter

4   abab, echo of the woman calling

5   caesuras, the speaker pausing to remember the past

6   9 11 13 14 15 16/1 2 3 4 5 6 7 8 10 12/insistence/vain hope destroyed or sorrow.

7   end, thorn/norward

Poetry toolbox 2

1   The following poem has been annotated with comments you could have made:

> I ate and ate my fill,
> Yet my mouth waters still;
> To-morrow night I will buy more:' and kissed her:
> 'Have done with sorrow;
> I'll bring you plums to-morrow
> Fresh on <u>their mother twigs</u>, ——————————— *1 unified*
> Cherries worth getting;
> You cannot think what fits
> <u>My teeth have met in</u>,   *10 luxurious*
> What melons <u>ice-cold</u> ——————————— *9 contrast*
> Piled on a <u>dish of gold</u>
> Too huge for me to hold,
> <u>What peaches with a velvet nap</u>, ——————— *7 opulence*
> Pellucid grapes without one seed:
> <u>Odorous indeed must be the mead</u>   *3 olfactory imagery*   *6 word association*
> Whereon they grow, and pure the <u>wave</u> they drink
> With lilies at the brink,
> And sugar-sweet their sap.
>
> Golden head by golden head,
> <u>Like two pigeons in one nest</u>   *2 united*
> Folded in each other's wings,
> They lay down in their <u>curtained bed</u>: ——— *4 secluded*
> <u>Like two blossoms</u> on one stem   *8 repeated images of unity*
> <u>Like two flakes</u> of new-fall'n snow, ——— *5 innocent*
> <u>Like two wands</u> of ivory
> <u>Tipped with gold for awful kings</u>.   *11 gold not positive*
> <u>Moon and stars gazed in at them</u>,   *3 positive natural imagery*
> <u>Wind sang to them</u> lullaby,
> <u>Lumbering owls</u> forbore to fly,   *3 negative natural imagery*
> <u>Not a bat flapped</u> to and fro
> Round their nest:
> <u>Cheek to cheek and breast to breast</u>
> <u>Locked together in one nest</u>. ——————— *11 finally unified*

Chaucer

1   human experience, (insert your tale – we shall use *The Wife of Bath*), character.

2   marriage and the experience of women in Chaucer's society.

3   wit, parody, irony, bawdiness

4   loquacity, honesty, brutality, argumentativeness etc.

5   For the Wife of Bath we could say that her main interest is authority over the male, and this is reflected in the treatment of the knight by the ladies in the court and how he acquiesces to the old woman and gives her mastery.

6   succinct and focused units of meaning

7   listen to a recording, read the poetry aloud.

Practical criticism: poetry

1   Analyse the words used in the title carefully. An anthem is a national song, one which brings a group of people together and gives them an identity. This poem is therefore a song which unites the soldiers. The word 'youth' suggests a hopeful and fulfilling future, yet the word 'doomed' contradicts this and introduces the idea of contrast – the soldiers, though young, are not 'youthful'. Their futures are marred with the constant threat of death which is all around them. The poem seems to highlight the barbaric circumstances of war, here emphasised by a comparison of the treatment of the dead soldiers on the battlefield and the Christian practices of burying the dead.

2   There is an extended metaphor running through this poem. The ugly burial of the dead soldiers is compared with the traditional ceremony at a Christian funeral. The poet selects various aspects of the service and finds a (usually disturbing) parallel in the battlefield. Words which indicate the metaphor are 'passing bells', 'prayers', 'bells', 'voice of mourning', 'bugles' and 'candles'. Every aspect of the funeral is therefore present, but the sound of shells replaces choirs of boys singing hymns, the only candle light is found in soldiers' eyes and the flowers and wreaths are represented by the patience and tenderness of those around them.

     A simile is used in the first line. The poet compares the death of the soldiers to that of slaughtered cattle. This suggests that the soldiers are killed in great numbers and that their bodies are treated like carcasses rather than with the respect that human bodies deserve.

     The last line introduces a new metaphor. The image of the drawn blinds has several implications. Obviously, for many soldiers, the blinds are drawn because they have lost their lives (traditional sign of mourning), life is now 'closed'. For those soldiers still alive, they may feel a 'drawing-down' of their own emotions – they have watched fellow soldiers die appalling, painful deaths and therefore they must need to separate themselves away from such horror simply to keep their sanity. The blinds close out the horrors of war.

3   The vocabulary used in the first stanza collocates strongly together, in that the words are negative and relate to the disturbance of the mind – 'monstrous', 'mourning', 'demented', 'wailing'. In the second stanza, the vocabulary again collocates strongly together – 'tenderness' and 'patient' – creating a different effect and atmosphere to the first stanza. It is as if the disturbing emotional state of Stanza One is resolved in Stanza Two. This is emphasised by the vocabulary of the two stanzas collocating weakly.

4   The connotations of the words used create sharp contrasts between a usual type of burial ceremony and the reality of death in war. The peaceful, religious, almost romantic connotations that we hold with choirs, bells, candles and flowers emphasise the harshness of the 'wailing shells' and sounds of the gunfire. The connotations of the choir boys' innocence and purity is extended to the soldiers – they are no more than boys themselves.

5   A striking use of phonology in the poem can be found in line three. The alliteration (r) and repetition of hard consonant sounds (t and p) of the 'stuttering rifles' rapid rattle' mirrors the sound of the repeated gun fire, creating onomatopoeia as the reader can hear the sound of the guns in the poem through the sound of the words used to describe it.

6   The guns are personified and given the human emotion of anger. This establishes the idea that, in angrily firing themselves, the guns are to blame for the deaths, rather than the soldiers. We are allowed to feel our compassion for the soldiers, forgetting that each one has killed another to save his own life.

7   Each stanza starts with a question which is then answered by the poet himself. The questions prompt the reader to consider carefully how the soldiers are treated in death and to judge their treatment against the norms of our society. To emphasise the tragedy of his answer, the poet uses repetition of negative words (nor and no) and words which emphasise limitation (only).

8   The first stanza contains eight lines, the second stanza contains six and the first questioning line of each stanza is longer than the others. This is intricately linked with the rhyme scheme.

9   The rhythm of the poem is agitated and inconsistent. This reflects the disturbing nature of the subject matter of the poem, not allowing the reader to feel at ease with the music of the language. The rhyme scheme of the poem is similarly unsettling. The first stanza consists of two sets of quatrains (ababcdcd) whilst the first four lines of the second stanza almost reflect the style of a sonnet (abba) with two rhyming couplets to complete the poem. The unease is also emphasised by the half rhymes in the poem (shells/shires).